THE OXYTOCIN FACTOR

THE OXYTOCIN FACTOR

Tapping the Hormone of Calm, Love, and Healing

Kerstin Uvnäs Moberg, M.D., Ph.D.

Foreword by Michel Odent

Translated from the Swedish by Roberta W. Francis

Drawings by Airi Iliste

The Oxytocin Factor
Tapping the hormone of calm, love, and healing

First published in the United States by Da Capo Press
A Member of the Perseus Books Group

This paperback edition first published in Great Britain by Pinter & Martin Ltd 2011

ISBN 978-1-905177-34-9

British Library Cataloguing-in-Publication Data
A catalogue record for this book is available from the British Library.

Designed by C. Cairl Design

Set in 12-point Adobe Garamond by the Perseus Books Group

Printed and bound in the EU by TJ International Ltd, Padstow, Cornwall

Pinter & Martin Ltd
6 Effra Parade
London SW2 1PS
www.pinterandmartin.com

CONTENTS ❦

FOREWORD

Professor Kerstin Uvnäs Moberg, of the prestigious Karolinska Institute in Stockholm, is the symbol of recent scientific advances influencing the future of childbirth.

The importance of many scientific advances is often ignored at the present time. This is the case with a whole generation of research concluding that the main maternal birth hormone is also the main hormone of love. Oxytocin, the hormone necessary for labour contractions including the delivery of the placenta, plays a crucial role in maternal behaviour. In fact, it is involved in all facets of love.

Niles Newton already anticipated the behavioural effects of oxytocin half a century ago.[1] However, it was not until 1979 when Cort Pedersen and Arthur Prange reported the evidence of such effects in their historical experiment.[2] To

1 Newton N. *Maternal Emotions*. Hoeber. New York 1955.
2 Pederson CA, Prange A. Induction of maternal behavior in virgin rats after intracerebroventricular administration of oxytocin. Proceedings of the National Academy of Sciences of the USA. 1979; 76;6661-6665.

induce maternal love, they injected oxytocin directly into the brain of virgin rats, instead of intravenously. Their research stimulated countless further studies of the many effects of oxytocin, particularly those by Kerstin Uvnäs Moberg and her team.

The general public had to wait several decades for this book wherein Kerstin Uvnäs Moberg, a prominent physiologist and a mother, explains the importance of both published studies and studies in progress. Her fascinating synthesis increases our understanding of the behavioural effects of oxytocin and of the interaction between oxytocin and stress hormones.

The applications for our current knowledge of oxytocin release are broad. This hormone is never released in isolation, but is always a component of a complex hormonal balance. This is why love has many facets. For example, just after birth or during breastfeeding, oxytocin release is associated with the release of prolactin, the "motherhood" hormone. The combination of these two hormones facilitates the expression of maternal love. Love of a sexual partner is another facet of love, but without a similar release of prolactin.

This significant research clearly belongs in the framework of the phenomenon I called the scientification of love.[3] Until recently love was a topic for poets, novelists or philosophers. Today, as Kerstin Uvnäs Moberg demonstrates, love is a subject for scientific disciplines as diverse as ethology (the objective study of behaviours), animal

3 Odent M. *The Scientification of Love*. Free Association Books. London 1999.

experimentation, a branch of epidemiology that explores the long-term consequences of events at the beginning of life ("Primal Health Research"), and the study of the behavioural effects of hormones involved in different sexual experiences. All these studies confirm the importance of the primal period, particularly the time surrounding birth. They provide answers to the question: "How does the capacity to love develop?" Traditionally, it has been commonplace to promote the importance of love, and to describe its multiple facets, without raising this fundamental question.

The significance of these issues concerns us all, because for the first time in history most women give birth without releasing a 'cocktail of love hormones'. Many women all over the world receive a drip of synthetic oxytocin as a substitute for the natural hormone their pituitary gland cannot easily release. In huge populations such as China and a great part of Latin America the caesarean is already the more common way to have a baby.[4] In other words, love hormones have been made redundant, at a global level, in the critical period surrounding birth.

We thank Kerstin Uvnäs Moberg for this valuable contribution to popular science and our understanding of human nature.

Michel Odent
April 2011

---

4 Odent M. *The Caesarean*. Free Association Books. London 2004.

ACKNOWLEDGMENTS ❧

I am very grateful to the people who have contributed to this book's existence. I thank my colleague, Professor Göran Nilsson, without whose encouragement I would not have begun the writing, and Roberta W. Francis, my friend and translator of the original Swedish text. These collaborations made my writing task both stimulating and enjoyable.

I also deeply appreciate the colleagues, doctoral candidates, and postdoctoral assistants who were my coworkers in the research that serves as the primary basis for this book. The group includes physicians, physiotherapists, behavioral researchers, psychologists, nutritionists, midwives, veterinarians, and agronomists. Our common cause is the scientific exploration that in recent years has cast more and more light on the workings of oxytocin. Many thanks for your enjoyable and inspiring collaboration.

I express my gratitude as well to the friends and family who have helped me during this time. I give special thanks to and for my children, Jenny, Anders, Wilhelm, and Axel, who by coming into the world set me on the right track.

Kerstin Uvnäs Moberg

INTRODUCTION ❧
A NEGLECTED SIDE OF LIFE

When we think about our lives, we usually think in terms of opposites, such as good and bad, light and dark, male and female, sun and moon. Whatever the reasons for this may be, our way of thinking in opposites is so ingrained that we rarely, if ever, notice it. Our scientific method, especially, is shaped by this style of thinking. Despite this, there are areas of knowledge in which only one of two poles is expressly articulated or engages our curiosity.

In physiology, the branch of medicine that attempts to describe how living animals function, we have for many years devoted a vast amount of attention to the physiology of exertion and stress, in large part through exploring the so-called fight or flight reaction. In this very well-known response, we and other mammals position ourselves to deal with stressful situations by either striking out or running away. We become angry, or afraid, or both. Our blood pressure goes up, and our digestive system, including the process of storing nutrition, comes to a virtual halt. We react more quickly and become less sensitive to pain. All the body's energy is focused on defending against the threat (real or imagined) that we are facing. Just as Popeye eats spinach and becomes the world's strongest man, people and other mammals under the influence of the fight or flight reaction have more than ordinary powers for a short time. Our bodies serve up an internal "power drink" in the form of hormones and signaling substances (called neurotransmitters).

The neglected physiological pattern that I will describe in this book is the opposite pole to the fight or flight reaction. Like most other mammals, we humans are able not only to mobilize when danger threatens but also to enjoy the good things in life, to relax, to bond, to heal. The fight or flight pattern has an opposite not only in the events of our lives but also in our biochemical system. This book deals with the other end of the seesaw, the body's own system for calm and connection.

This calm and connection system is associated with trust and curiosity instead of fear, and with friendliness instead of anger. The heart and circulatory system slow down as the digestion fires up. When peace and calm prevail, we let our defenses down and instead become sensitive, open, and interested in others around us. Instead of tapping the internal "power drink," our bodies offer a ready-made healing nectar. Under its influence, we see the world and our fellow humans in a positive light; we grow, we heal. This response is also the effect of hormones and signaling substances, but until now, the connections among these vital physiological effects have not been fully recognized and studied.

The neglect of this system tells us much about the values that underlie scientific research. The calm and connection system is certainly as important for survival as the system for defense and exertion, and it is equally as complex. Nevertheless, the stress system is explored much more frequently. For example, in research on the autonomic nervous system (the part of the nervous system that regulates involuntary body functions), only 10 percent of studies deal with the parasympathetic part, which is involved with rest and growth, and the remaining 90 percent are devoted to the sympathetic part, which is active in defense and stress. Many scientific conferences are held on the topics of stress and pain, but very few deal with calm, rest, and well-being.

One reason why research has been so slanted may be that goal-directed activity is emphasized so strongly in our culture. We are used to defining activity as something moving, something we can see. But many of the calm and connection system's processes and effects are not visible to the naked eye. They also occur slowly and gradually, and they are not as easy to isolate or define as are the more dramatic actions involving attack and defense. Just as Nasruddin in the Sufi tale searched for his key where he could see best, not where he had lost it, physiologists have studied the clearly visible fight or flight mechanism but have been less able to perceive the more hidden and subtle calm and connection system.

The calm and connection system is most often at work when the body is at rest. In this apparent stillness, an enormous amount of activity is taking place, but it is not directed to movement or bursts of effort. This system instead helps the body to heal and grow. It changes nourishment to energy, storing it up for later use. Body and mind become calm. In this state, we have greater access to our internal resources and creativity. The ability to learn and to solve problems increases when we are not under stress.

I believe that it is extremely important to increase our understanding of the physical and psychological workings of this antithesis to the fight or flight system. We need both, since for each individual in each situation there is an optimal way to react. But it is now well known that long-term stress can produce a variety of psychological and physical problems. If we are to be healthy in the long run, the two systems must be kept in balance.

The line of research a scientist chooses to explore is not the result of chance. I believe we select our direction of inquiry based on a combination of personal experiences, the spirit of the times, and the political climate in our profession. Unconscious memories and experiences also play a role, perhaps more than we suspect. Out of this mix, we set up hypotheses that we work to prove or disprove, and we formulate questions that we try to answer.

For these reasons, an interest in the physiology of performance, exertion, and defense has dominated existing scientific knowledge and current research to an extent that we

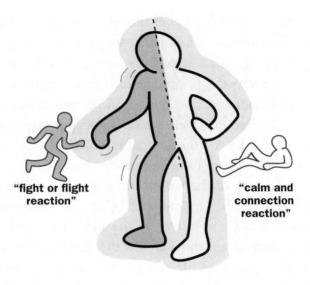

FIGURE I.1 We need a balance between exertion and stress (fight or flight reaction) and rest and recovery (calm and connection reaction).

do not always recognize. This way of looking at things, or shall I say those blinders, has until now kept those of us who work in the medical sciences from seeing the calm and connection response as a separate and valuable physiological system. Thus, for me, studying this system has involved an element of swimming against the tide with respect to the political mainstream in my profession.

The reasons that I chose this line of research are in part personal. My experience as the mother of four children has raised some interesting questions. In pregnancy, nursing, and close contact with my children, I experienced a state diametrically opposed to the stress I was familiar with in

connection with life's other challenges. I was aware that the
psychophysiological conditions associated with pregnancy
and nursing fostered something entirely different from
challenge, competition, and performance. Inspired more
than two decades ago to explore this life experience scientifically, I learned that there is a key biological marker—the
subject of this book—on the trail to a physiological explanation of this state of calm and connection.

In some parts of the world, peace and calm have been
traditionally valued as a mode of being worth cultivating.
Chinese, Hindu, and other cultures have developed techniques to help attain this state. In the search for pathways
to a higher quality of life and greater well-being, meditation, yoga, t'ai chi, and other such practices are being
explored with much interest today in the Western world.

The more stressful and fragmented our modern world
becomes, the more we become mindful of our need for
calm and connection. This longing finds expression in a
questioning of our hectic lifestyles and a conscious pursuit
of avenues to serenity and comfortable personal relationships. But when this need is more unconscious and unrecognized, it can generate different types of personal
responses, some of which are effective solutions and others
unhealthy in the long run.

For instance, abundant food, especially food rich in fat,
is calming and conducive to a good sleep, but there are
obvious unfortunate consequences if we habitually soothe
ourselves in this way. Alcohol also makes us calm and
drowsy, and many people use it as a way to wind down after

a stressful day. This, too, can lead to problems. People who suffer from stress, anxiety, or even depression can take medications prescribed by a doctor, but even the newest drugs, which are not considered to be directly habit-forming, can have unwanted side effects.

Some people find that physical exercise gives them a pleasant feeling of peace and calm, while also producing the positive effect of weight control. Some people regularly undergo various alternative medicine treatments—such as acupuncture, acupressure, massage, and different types of energy treatments—not only to find relief from physical symptoms but because they notice that it helps calm them. Many people find serenity and relaxation in spiritual practices such as meditative stillness and prayer.

In the coming chapters, we will see that what seem to be completely different physical and mental routes to relaxation and well-being actually have certain similarities. They all seem to work by activating the same internal system in our bodies with the assistance of an extraordinary biochemical called *oxytocin*.

The analysis contained in these chapters is supported by the results of my own and others' research. Over the years, I have seen evolve a network of colleagues with a similar interest in these processes and a shared conviction that this research has important implications for health and well-being. This network includes not only professional colleagues and graduate-level researchers but also interested members of the public who have given us many leads and have shared valuable experiences.

My line of reasoning about oxytocin's effects is based on animal experiments and observations and measurements with humans. From these findings, I make assumptions and propose hypotheses about things that we have not yet been able to research scientifically. I do this to make the "big picture" visible, to describe the calm and connection system as a whole, even though research has still not fully explored this territory. By linking oxytocin with the broad array of physiological effects that I call the *calm and connection system*, I am building a case on persuasive but sometimes circumstantial evidence. It's like putting together a puzzle that has some missing pieces; by joining the pieces we do have, we can take a few steps back, see the picture from a larger perspective, and thereby get an idea of how the final calm and connection system is most likely going to look.

This short book cannot by any means be a full summary of all the research that has been done in this area. Instead, with certain scientific results as a starting point, I take the liberty of speculating about our need for calm and connection, the way these effects are produced, and the positive influence they have on our health. These, I believe, are important issues that scientists must explore further.

Parts One and Two describe this interconnected system and the specific physiological processes that make it work. Part Three spells out some of oxytocin's powerful effects. Part Four shows situations in which it is triggered, and Part Five describes some of the many ways these effects can be used to achieve calm, healing, and growth.

PART ONE

The Calm and Connection System

Oxytocin

In 1906, the English researcher Sir Henry Dale discovered a substance in the pituitary gland that could speed up the birthing process. He named it oxytocin, from the Greek words for "quick" and "childbirth labor." Later, he found that it also promoted the expulsion of breast milk. Now it appears that oxytocin plays a much larger physiological role than previously recognized, since under many circumstances it has the ability to produce the effects that we associate with the state of calm and connection.

When I began the work described in this book, I had already experienced a systematic change in my behavior and way of thinking in connection with pregnancy, childbirth, and nursing. I found explanations for this in the scientific literature about oxytocin. The materials I studied also described animal experiments showing that oxytocin in various ways increased the mother's interaction with her young and created a bond between them. Could it be, I wondered, that oxytocin also affects human beings in such ways, as well as in other ways that we are not aware of, both physically and psychologically?

I became curious and read everything about oxytocin that I could get my hands on. I learned that it is not simply a hormone that circulates through the bloodstream to influence various functions; it appears also in the brain as a neurotransmitter, or signaling substance, working through a large network of nerves that connect with many different areas of that organ. In these ways, I discovered, oxytocin is able to influence many vital operations in the body. The same brain and nervous system that produce the fight or flight mechanism sometimes generate entirely opposite responses when oxytocin is involved.

An Age-Old Pair

Oxytocin was one of the first hormones whose chemical construction was mapped in the mid–twentieth century. The substance is composed of nine amino acids and is closely related in structure to another biochemical, vasopressin, differing from it by only two amino acids.

From an evolutionary perspective, oxytocin and vasopressin are ancient substances. These two molecules have been present in the chain of animal development for millions of years. Oxytocin is found, entirely unchanged chemically, in all species of mammals. Except for a slight difference in molecular structure in a few species, the same is true of vasopressin. Birds and reptiles produce similar substances, mesotocin and vasotocin, that correspond to the ancient pair, and even the earthworm has its oxytocin to stimulate egg laying.

The fact that oxytocin and vasopressin have existed for such a long time in animals indicates that the substances are of fundamental importance and perform vital functions for both humans and other animals.

Not Just a Female Hormone

Vasopressin has long been recognized as an important element in the fight or flight mechanism in mammals since, among other things, it keeps the body's fluid volume at a balanced level and helps to raise blood pressure. Along with more familiar substances, such as adrenaline, vasopressin is one ingredient in the internal "power drink" that stimulates defensive actions and the physical and behavioral adaptations needed for struggle and boundary setting, behaviors often associated with the male sex.

Oxytocin, on the other hand, has traditionally been regarded as a female hormone because it was discovered in connection with birth and nursing. As I began investigating oxytocin, however, I soon began to suspect that its role was significantly greater than formerly thought. It appeared to be involved not only with birth, nursing, and maternal behavior but also with other, as yet unclear, functions. I therefore launched a series of experiments with my colleagues to explore the effects of oxytocin from a more general perspective.

These experiments were generally performed by administering oxytocin to rats and then studying which behaviors and bodily functions it influenced. In many of the experiments the rats were asleep, but some of the tests required that they be awake. (In my judgment, these experiments have not been painful for the animals.) It has subsequently been possible to verify certain results of the animal experiments by observing and examining humans, for example, nursing women.

Oxytocin is produced by males and females in many different situations, and our experiments show that its effects are evident in both sexes. In one series of studies, we show that oxytocin can easily be released to a similar extent in both sexes through pleasant warmth and rhythmic touch. The oxytocin system is thus by no means strictly a female system, but has crucial significance for both sexes in humans and other mammals.

A connection does exist between oxytocin and the female sex hormone, estrogen, and between vasopressin and the male sex hormone, testosterone. That will be discussed later. Oxytocin's effects make us think of qualities traditionally seen as feminine: receptivity, closeness, openness to relationship, and the giving of nurturing and nourishment. Identification of these attributes primarily with the female sex is less common today since many men are also successfully acknowledging and developing these qualities.

Although we cannot translate our experimental results directly from animals to people, nature has provided us with a "free experiment" for examining the effects of oxytocin on humans. Since a large amount of oxytocin is released in nursing women over a limited period, we can obtain direct information about oxytocin's effects by studying these women. To take advantage of this opportunity, I began a long-term and rewarding collaboration with midwives at the Karolinska Hospital in Stockholm. We measured nursing women's oxytocin levels and correlated them with various physiological indicators, such as blood pressure, as well as with the women's own descriptions of the intensity of various feelings, such as anxiety. Oxytocin levels are naturally influenced by various factors in each individual, such as heredity and life situation. Our experimental results showed, however, that the level of oxytocin in the blood during nursing was correlated with the mothers' physical manifestations and subjective experiences of calm, lack of stress, and ability to interact with their babies.

Later experiments with cows that were suckling their calves also revealed nearly the same pattern, correlating increased oxytocin levels with greater calmness and more interaction between the animals. These results further support the premise that oxytocin produces the same effects in all mammals.

How Can Oxytocin Do So Much?

A criticism often directed at the concept of a calm and connection system in which oxytocin plays the key role is that it is improbable that one substance could do so many different things. This skepticism is understandable, since we know that animals lacking the gene for oxytocin production (for example, the laboratory-bred "knock-out mouse") can still survive. Recent research has shown, however, that such animals have great difficulty in coping with an unfamiliar environment. If placed in a cage different from the type they grew up in, they lose certain basic skills, as well as the ability to learn new skills. They also display an abnormal reaction to stress.

It is important to recognize that oxytocin is seldom the final link in the many chain-reaction effects that it can trigger. Oxytocin fuels a coordinating and modulating system that works through the bloodstream and through many nerve branches linking to important control areas of the brain. It influences and is influenced by other classic neurotransmitters, such as serotonin, dopamine, and noradrenaline.

The feedback mechanisms in the oxytocin system enable oxytocin-producing cells both to receive and to deliver communications through nerve and chemical contact with the surrounding environment. Since information is transmitted to these cells from the body's outside, inside, and sensory organs, the release of oxytocin is easy to promote. Interestingly, even thoughts, associations, and memories can set the system into operation (as explained in Chapter 7).

The Big Picture and the Details

In our research, we have examined the interactions of multiple systems. It is not productive in this work to select in advance one specific effect of oxytocin and then study how it appears at, for example, the cellular level; if we do, we are sure to miss the fact that oxytocin's different effects actually create a pattern, a tapestry of reciprocal connections. We must continuously broaden our perspective to make sense of the details. In my research about the overall system that produces calm and connection, therefore, I have not used the exclusively close-up focus that I would employ in studying, for example, the functioning of cells and genes. But this research is no less objective because of that.

When you study an ant in the grass, you first see the ant from up close, with all its legs and antennae, and see how it carries a blade of grass on its back. If you lift the lens somewhat, you see the lawn that is the ant's whole world, but you no longer see the ant. If you observe the picture from higher and higher, you see that the lawn is part of a landscape, which is part of a country, which is part of a continent, and little by little you come to see the whole globe. Purposefulness and organization are required in all these observations, whether of the structure of the blade of grass or the quality of the lawn, but different research objectives require different methods and concepts. If we see the researcher as a photographer, she must use a magnifying lens to study the ant, a wide-angle lens to study the lawn.

It is important to understand that the calm and connection system is composed of an ingenious pattern of nerves and hormones that *together* trigger many different effects. It is this pattern that must be studied. When we examine life's functions, it is not sufficient to study only the separate parts, such as cells and molecules, for then we will lose the big picture. We must from time to time stand up and observe the whole pattern before we can go back to examine the details more closely.

2

The Environmental Context

A growing understanding of ecology and feedback systems has led us to see that every living organism is in constant contact with its surrounding environment and continuously influenced by it. Tactile input, body posture, ambient temperature, and hunger or fullness are only a few of the immense number of variables constantly providing information that influences our physical and mental functioning without our awareness.

We tend to think that our biological rhythms are independent of the environment, but many of them were originally acquired through interaction with the outside world. It is not by chance that women's menstrual cycles and the moon's phases correspond, any more than it is a coincidence that all people have a built-in diurnal rhythm of approximately the same length. At one time, moonlight and sunlight actually controlled such functions directly, but through evolution these rhythms have become incorporated into our biological systems.

As the concept of the organism as a holistic entity is beginning to enter medical practice and literature, it has become an accepted truth that body and mind function interdependently. The mind-body connection we have paid most attention to, however, is that of fear and the fight or flight reaction. We are only now recognizing and exploring the mental and physiological interactions involved in responses of calming, relaxing, and connecting.

Constant Stress—Rare Calm

If it is true that we are continuously influenced by our environment, what happens if the environment's signals are radically altered? What if the balance between challenging situations and comforting circumstances is chronically changed? Won't this shift trigger large physiological effects and disturb our inner sense of equanimity?

Complaints about the amount of stress in modern Western culture are so common that we hardly hear them anymore. Today, the pressure to achieve is enormous. The tempo is fast, the flood of information is heavy, and the competition for jobs is tough. The barrage of sights, smells, and especially sounds is constant. There is no doubt that the stress-related fight or flight system inside us has been activated to the point of overload.

Meanwhile, the traditional situations that tend to promote peacefulness, relaxation, and intimacy have become

FIGURE 2.1 We need balance between pressure and calm, stress and relaxation.

less common in our society; and the less often they occur, the less often our inner biological system of calm and connection is activated.

Touch, as we will see, appears to be one of the strongest sources of input to the calm and connection system. When a family or another group of people does something together, touch, smell, and other senses play a natural part in their interactions. As a result of modern cultural trends toward greater independence and fewer daily communal activities, such sensory impressions decrease. This altered pattern reduces the activity of the calm and connection system and ultimately poses a danger to our health.

Experiences that feed this system have, it seems to me, diminished nearly as dramatically as input to the stress-related system has grown. This change can have serious consequences for our well-being, since the body's ability to relax and recharge also moderates our physical and psychological reactions to stress itself. Many illnesses are caused at least in part by stress; therefore, if stress increases without the corresponding counterbalance of healing and relaxation, our health is jeopardized.

We need calm and connection not only to avoid illness, but also to enjoy life, to feel curious, optimistic, creative. These qualities are hard to measure scientifically. What research does show, however, is that concentration and learning are improved by a peaceful environment and nurturing relationships. Children under stress have a harder time learning than those who are calm and secure.

In Search of Calm

Fortunately, many of us more or less intuitively understand that we need periodically to replenish our dwindling reservoirs of calm, and we search for various ways to feel well and happy despite the stressful environment we find ourselves in.

When overstressed people seek help from traditional medical practitioners, they are often disappointed. Many people with chronic stomachaches, for example, are not satisfied until they receive some alternative form of therapy, which sometimes actually provides a cure. The great need to balance stress with relaxation and physical contact may be one reason why such treatments, though generally not covered by insurance, are thriving and growing in scope. Something is clearly missing in the high-tech care most often offered today, something that can apparently be found instead in alternative treatment techniques. It is obvious that patients whose illnesses are connected with their life situations and experiences may not always receive the right diagnosis if the conclusions are drawn only from blood tests and laboratory results.

Many people attend courses in stress management or explore alternative medicine treatments in which touch is an important component. When touch is made important in care, it makes the people involved important: the caregivers who touch and those who need touch because they are sick or in discomfort. Perhaps in the future such therapies will become an accepted ally to traditional medical care by adding needed balance to the technical apparatus and laboratory tests with a complement of nearness and contact. Chapters 9, 11, 12, and 13 deal in more detail with the significance of touch and close relationship for the oxytocin system.

Insight from Caregivers

I regularly lecture to physical therapists, nurses, midwives, and other caregivers, as well as to psychologists and physicians. When I do so, I often have a strong sense that my audience not only understands what I am talking about but also welcomes my message. Health care professionals involved in the direct care of patients are glad to hear a definition of the calm and connection system and its physical and mental benefits, because most of them are aware from experience that these effects exist. They know, too, that with their own hands they can connect with their patients and provide them with a sense of calm, but they have not seen this effect described in the literature as a physiological phenomenon. Instead, the positive results of the calm and connection system have been attributed to a purely psychological effect, or, in earlier times, a "healing," or even a miracle.

When what these caregivers do in their daily work is shown to have a name and a scientific basis, their sense of professional identity is strengthened. They understand that what they have can be described as a "physiological skill," that is, an ability to activate the body's own mechanisms for promoting growth and healing. The acknowledgment of these skills is much needed. The prevailing belief in the technological and pharmacological elements of medicine is so enormous that the confidence of these professionals in their own care giving as a therapeutic method has been eroded, even though many patients who have recovered through this type of care can testify to its importance and effectiveness.

When I name some of oxytocin's effects to people who know the characteristics of the calm and connection system in practice, they can often fill in the rest. It is obvious to them that certain effects, such as calmness, lower blood pressure, and a higher tolerance for pain, are associated. Many physical therapists have also seen that the effects obtained after several treatments are long lasting, and can then be maintained with fewer, less frequent sessions. As we shall see in Chapter 7, this pattern conforms well with the profile of oxytocin's effects.

I nearly always find ideas for new research when I lecture to groups of caregivers, thanks to the questions and comments I get from the audience. This feedback convinces me that without a doubt there are elements of the calm and connection system that have yet to be explored.

The Need for More Research

The physiological pattern described in this book involves not the discovery of a new nervous system, but a new understanding of how the environment influences our existing nervous system to operate so that calm and connection are created. I hope that this calm and connection mechanism will soon be commonly accepted as a distinct, active physiological system, and not viewed only as the absence of stress. The operation of this system can counter the effects of constant stress and strain. The brain can "reverse engines" and begin to work in another direction to achieve calm, rest, and healing without the need for medications or complicated technology.

The need to increase research into oxytocin and the various therapies that seem to lead to its release should be obvious. The calm and connection mechanism is an important and ingenious system in our bodies that influences growth, healing, the recharge of energy, and social interaction. I am convinced that increased knowledge about oxytocin will over time explain how various alternative medicine techniques work.

In addition, knowledge about oxytocin will also make it possible for us to find new ways to foster our well-being in today's complicated and demanding society. Such knowledge will help us better understand the need to create a balance between activity and rest, between outer-directed work and inner-directed reflection, between reaching out for contact and setting boundaries. We will then more likely choose lifestyles, occupations, and activities that will enable us to cope with our stressful environment without losing this balance. This is the way to better health, both for individuals and societies.

❧ 3

An Essential Balance

This book deals with a physiological mechanism that is in some ways like the fight or flight reaction and in other ways quite the reverse. It operates not to mobilize us for defense, but to slow us down to promote growth and recovery. Although we easily perceive the active response, we discover the other pattern in the same manner that a photograph is produced from a negative. When white becomes black and black becomes white, what we didn't see before becomes obvious to us. So it is with the system for calm and connection. Everyone is aware of it instinctively, but few of us are used to looking at it so clearly that it becomes something unto itself, the reverse image of the defense and stress system.

Fight or Flight

Thanks to an ingenious system of signals, the human body is built to interact with its environment in a way that at each second and in every situation is optimal for our individual survival and thereby the continuation of our species. Stress, physical and psychological, causes the body to mobilize its available energy so that we can deal with a challenging situation until it improves and we can catch our breath.

We react in acutely stressful situations much the same way as the first members of our species did. Now as then, our physiological system musters all its innate intelligence in the interest of our survival. It works in two major ways: Either we actively defend ourselves against what threatens us, or we run away from it. (In certain circumstances, we may resort to a response of passivity, a human version of some animals' ability to play dead.)

Think about how you felt the last time you became really afraid or angry. Do you remember how your heart began to beat faster and harder? Under stress, both the frequency and the intensity of the heartbeat increase, thereby increasing the blood flow in the muscles. In addition, your liver released stored energy in the form of glucose, which provided extra fuel for those muscles. We might say that, as your body prepared to function at its maximum capacity, you became stronger for a while.

But this was not the only physical reaction that increased your body's capacity to perform. Your air passages dilated and you breathed more rapidly; in this way, you increased your body's ventilation and elevated the oxygen level in your blood. Your pupils widened so that you could see better in all directions and more easily identify possible danger.

Someone who saw you in that condition might also note that your skin color changed. Because of reduced or increased blood circulation in the skin, you may have become pale from fear or flushed with anger, depending on the situation. What was not visible, however, was that the circulation in your stomach and intestines was also altered, and your entire digestive apparatus was affected. Cutting back on the blood supply to and activity in certain parts of the body is one of the organism's wise ways of saving energy so that it can use it where it is most needed. It is not important to use energy to digest food and store nutrition when survival itself may be at stake.

In defensive or stressful situations, the sympathetic part of the autonomic nervous system (which regulates involuntary bodily functions) is activated, leading to increased heart activity and elevated blood flow to the muscles involved in movement. In this way, the conditions for heavy exertion are improved. The substance noradrenaline plays an important role in making this happen. The adrenal gland also becomes more active, secreting the stress hormones adrenaline and cortisol into the blood. (Part Two explains in greater detail how the central nervous system functions to produce these reactions.)

Calm and Connection

Just as we have all experienced how stress, fear, or anger acts upon us physically, each of us also knows how we feel when the opposite happens.

Think of yourself after a good meal. You lean back in your chair and may even feel a strong urge to lie down on the sofa for a little nap. You may notice that you are less upset about your problems than you were before the meal. The aches and pains you have may feel more tolerable now. You feel peaceful, and you may smile contentedly. You may want to pull back from things for a while, or you may feel a sense of closeness to the people around you and want to open to the nearness and touch of someone's embrace. At this moment, you are not stressed at all. You are experiencing the state of calm and connection.

Life treats us with many opportunities to enjoy this condition. When we lie down to sunbathe on a warm beach, it is the calm and connection mechanism that causes us to enjoy it as we do. In the same way, a warm bath generates a feeling of peaceful well-being. A massage gives us rosy skin and allows the body, including the face muscles, to relax and rest. Meditation lowers the stress level and is often spoken of as the path to inner calm. Breast-feeding women relax into physical and emotional closeness with their nursing infants, becoming more engaged and open to contact. Even the little child sucking on the nipple becomes peaceful.

All these pleasant stimuli trigger the brain's release of oxytocin, which plays a key role in promoting the body's calm and connection response.

As mentioned above, the "cradle" of oxytocin research was the discovery of its existence in connection with childbirth and breast-feeding. Today, we know that this important biochemical, found in both sexes, plays a key role in many other situations and conditions, which, despite their different appearances, have a common denominator: They are all characterized by peacefulness, relaxation, and a feeling of contentment.

Contrary to the fight or flight reaction, the calm and connection response is marked by *lower* blood pressure and *lower* levels of the stress hormone cortisol. The appetite may increase, and digestion, especially the absorption and storing of nutrition in the body's fat depots, becomes more effective.

OPPOSITE REACTIONS

The fight or flight reaction is marked by
- increased heart rate and pumping volume;
- elevated blood pressure;
- increased blood circulation in the muscles;
- extra fuel from release of glucose from the liver; and
- a higher level of stress hormones.

The calm and connection reaction is marked by
- lowered blood pressure and heart rate;
- increased circulation in the skin and mucous membranes (seen, for example, as rosy skin in the face and other parts of the body);
- lowered level of stress hormones; and
- more effective digestion, nutritional uptake and storage (seen over time as increased weight).

Blood circulation increases in the skin and mucous membranes and decreases in the muscles.

Interestingly, many of these changes not only happen immediately but also persist over time. Thus, activities that influence the body in this way are significant from a health perspective, since maintaining blood pressure and nutritional uptake at optimal levels keeps the body in good condition.

A Necessary Balance

It is important to emphasize that both the fight or flight reaction and the condition of calm and connection are essential to life. Precisely like other animals, we humans must have the ability to meet challenges and mobilize all our powers to take whatever action is needed at a given time. Likewise, we also need the opposite. The body needs to digest food, replenish its stores, and heal itself. We must be able to take in information, express feelings, be open and curious, and establish contact with other people. It is this ability that enables us to recover after more or less challenging incidents or periods.

As noted earlier, the two conditions of fight or flight and calm and connection tend to operate in balance, as if on a see-saw. When we contentedly digest food, we seldom experience agitation, anger, or stress. When we are wound up, angry, or hurried, digestion slows down and we feel less sociable. One mechanism does not exclude the other, but either one of them can temporarily dominate.

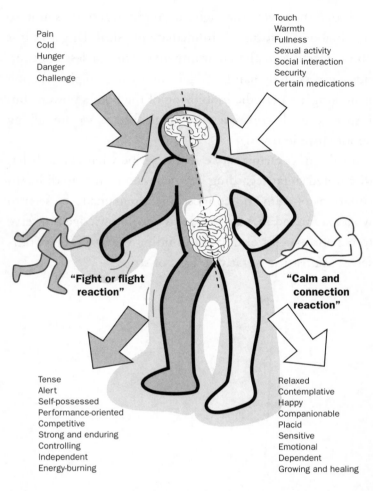

Pain
Cold
Hunger
Danger
Challenge

Touch
Warmth
Fullness
Sexual activity
Social interaction
Security
Certain medications

"Fight or flight reaction"

"Calm and connection reaction"

Tense
Alert
Self-possessed
Performance-oriented
Competitive
Strong and enduring
Controlling
Independent
Energy-burning

Relaxed
Contemplative
Happy
Companionable
Placid
Sensitive
Emotional
Dependent
Growing and healing

FIGURE 3.1   The two equally necessary physiological conditions: fight or flight and calm and connection.

Today, however, the fight or flight reaction is not so much about warding off immediate physical danger as it is about reacting to the environment's more or less continuously excessive demands. When the fight or flight reaction is no longer a periodic mobilizing of the body's powers, but instead a nearly constant physiological state, we are talking about chronic stress.

In the next chapters, we will describe what research has discovered so far regarding oxytocin and its role in different situations of calm and connection. It remains to be seen to what extent and in what ways this new knowledge can serve to benefit us—for example, in finding ways to protect ourselves against the negative effects of stress.

PART TWO

Oxytocin's Role in the
Brain and Nervous System

4

The Body's Control Centers

To understand the role oxytocin plays in producing calm and connection, it helps to have a basic knowledge of how the brain and nervous system are constructed. The following overview is much simplified in the interests of clarity and understanding. (Readers who already have a knowledge of anatomy and physiology can go directly to the next chapter without losing the thread of the discussion.)

The Central Nervous System

The central nervous system consists of the brain and the spinal cord; these are composed primarily of nerve cells, called neurons, which send and receive signals. Each neuron consists of a cell body with a number of protuberances. Those protuberances that send signals (often one long one per neuron) are called axons, and those that receive signals

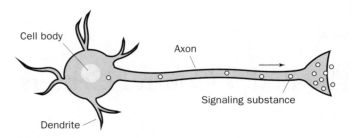

FIGURE 4.1   Neuron, or nerve cell.

are called dendrites. Each of us has more than 100 billion neurons.

A continuous exchange of information takes place between neurons. A single neuron can send and receive signals from 200,000 other neurons. When a nerve is activated, a weak electric current passes through it, and the slight negative charge normally found on the nerve cell's outside surface becomes positive for a brief time. This electric current runs with extreme rapidity along the nerve's length. When the impulse reaches the nerve ending, chemical messengers, known as signaling substances or neurotransmitters, are released.

The connection between two nerves or between a nerve and an organ is called a synapse. Receptors on the receiving nerve or organ function as contact points, somewhat like an electrical outlet in a wall. They take in the released signaling substances and begin a reaction inside the receiving cell so that the next nerve, gland, or muscle cell can be activated.

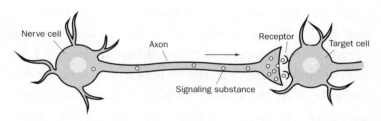

FIGURE 4.2   A synapse is the area between a nerve cell and a target cell (for example, another nerve cell) where the signaling substance is carried over from the sending cell to bind with receptors in the receiving cell.

The central nervous system exercises its astonishing control through the constant activity of weak electrical impulses. This control is exerted from different parts of the brain, which for purposes of this overview I'll describe as three levels—the upper level, or cortex; the lower brain; and the spinal cord.

The part of the brain usually seen as the highest level is called the cortical level, or cerebral cortex. The central nervous system also controls bodily processes from parts of the brain that, because they are older from an evolutionary perspective, are grouped together under the designation "lower brain level." This level includes the limbic system and the brain stem. The third and lowest level in the central nervous system is the spinal cord itself.

The different levels of the central nervous system correspond to different levels of control over the body. The cerebral cortex has an overall role: It serves as our memory center and the manager of conscious thought processes, such as the ability to plan and make associations. The cerebral cortex places humans in a different category from other animals. An area in the cortex's frontal lobe appears especially to be the seat of the highest functions of consciousness. The cerebral cortex is also important for registering our awareness of touch as well as for activating certain motions.

For the most part, however, the cerebral cortex is not responsible by itself for bodily activities. When it is engaged, we almost always see lower levels of the brain acting with it.

Most of what happens in the body is actually controlled at the level of the lower brain (limbic system and brain stem, see Figure 4.3). These lower levels are constantly active because they are what keeps us alive. They operate without the involvement of either our consciousness or our will. Heartbeat, breathing, and blood pressure are controlled from this level, especially from the brain stem. When you react to pain or when you become frightened, excited, or sexually aroused, this level is in charge. This control is exercised primarily through the activity of the hypothalamus and the amygdala, which will be described more fully later in this chapter. These two cell groups in the limbic system are of special importance for our experience of feelings and the resulting reactions of our bodies, all of which are the focus of this book.

The spinal cord can be seen as the link between the different parts of the body and the higher levels of the nervous system. In some cases, it transports nerve signals from the body's periphery to the brain; in others, the information goes out in the other direction from the brain or other parts of the nervous system. Various complicated activities are controlled directly from the spinal cord. One example is reflex action, as when you burn yourself on a hot surface and quickly pull your hand away without stopping to think about it. This reflex action, triggered by the skin's pain receptors, is controlled directly from the spinal cord, even before the message goes to the brain. With a possible burn, there is no time to lose. This third level of the nervous system also helps control blood pressure, activity in the gastrointestinal system, and the responses of our sex organs during sex.

Thus these levels of the central nervous system operate in a sort of hierarchy: The highest level has responsibility for the most subtle activities (thought, memory, and planning), the mid-level controls basic survival and reproduction, and the lowest level takes care of the most primitive functions (pain and other reflexes).

THE CENTRAL NERVOUS SYSTEM

1. Cerebral cortex
2. Lower brain level (consisting of the limbic system and the brain stem)
3. Spinal cord

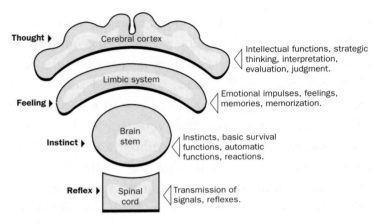

FIGURE 4.3   Schematic overview of the brain's levels of function.

The Peripheral Nervous System

In the peripheral nervous system (which is outside the central nervous system), are nerves that lead to and from the body's skin, muscles, and organs. Outgoing nerves are called motor nerves; incoming ones are called sensory nerves. The peripheral nervous system is commonly divided into consciously controlled (somatic) and automatically operating (autonomic) parts.

The Somatic Nervous System

When we move about, our skeletons and muscles are controlled through the central nervous system. Somatic nerves transport signals to the muscles with the help of a signaling substance called acetylcholine. These somatic nerves go out from the spinal cord, but they are also connected with the

THE PERIPHERAL NERVOUS SYSTEM

This system consists of nerves that go to and from the skin, muscles, and organs outside the central nervous system. It contains

- motor nerves, which transport signals outward from the brain to the muscles and other organs in the body;
- sensory nerves, which carry signals of sensation from the periphery (skin, muscles, various organs) to the brain;
- somatic nerves, which are voluntarily controlled; and
- autonomic nerves, which are not voluntarily controlled.

higher levels of the central nervous system. In this way, different levels of the nervous system may be involved at the same time in producing a particular motion.

When reflexes respond to dangerous outside stimuli, such as a hot surface, only the lowest level of the nervous system, the spinal cord, is involved. The higher levels are involved in acts that are controlled by thought and will, as when you decide to bend your leg or turn a page in this book.

The Autonomic Nervous System

Parallel to the somatic, or motor, nerves, which direct the motion of the skeleton and muscles, are the outgoing nerves

---

THE SOMATIC NERVOUS SYSTEM

1. Controls muscles
2. Produces both quick reflexes and more complicated voluntary movements
3. Uses acetylcholine as its primary signaling substance

---

in the autonomic nervous system. These work involuntarily, without our needing to do anything, to control heartbeat, circulation, digestion (including the rippling motions of the intestines, called peristalsis), and breathing.

The autonomic nervous system in turn is subdivided into the sympathetic and parasympathetic systems. The sympathetic nerves go out from the part of the spinal cord that corresponds with the breast and groin areas. The most important substance that transports signals from the sympathetic nervous system to the affected organs is called noradrenaline.

The nerves in the parasympathetic system leave from the brain stem and converge in the vagus nerve, the large nerve that leads to several of the body's internal organs, including the gastrointestinal system. Some parasympathetic nerves also emanate from the lowest part of the spinal cord. In this system, as in the somatic system, messages are transmitted by the signaling substance acetylcholine.

In a sense, the sympathetic and the parasympathetic systems have opposite functions and balance each other. For example, the sympathetic system is engaged in the so-called

THE AUTONOMIC NERVOUS SYSTEM

1. Controls the activity of internal organs, for example, the heart, circulatory system, gastrointestinal system, lungs;
2. Consists of the sympathetic and parasympathetic nervous systems; and
3. Contains incoming sensory nerves.

Sympathetic nerves
- are active in movement;
- govern the fight or flight reaction's physical responses;
- go out from the spinal cord; and
- use noradrenaline as the primary signaling substance.

Parasympathetic nerves
- are active in the digestive process;
- are associated with the calm and connection mechanism's physical adaptations;
- go out from the brain stem and the lower spinal cord; and
- use acetylcholine as the primary signaling substance.

fight or flight response and produces, among other things, a rise in pulse rate and blood pressure. The parasympathetic system supports, among other things, digestion and the storage of nutrients, which slow down in the fight or flight

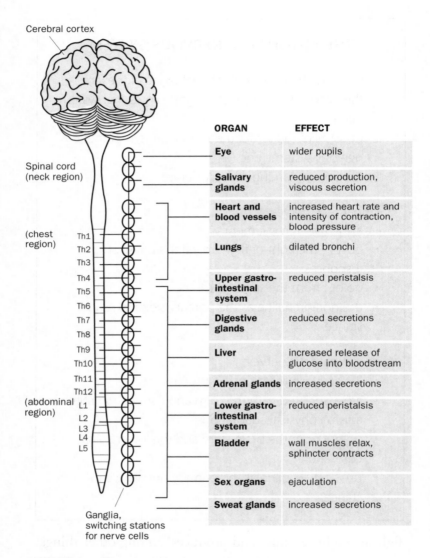

FIGURE 4.4   The sympathetic nervous system.

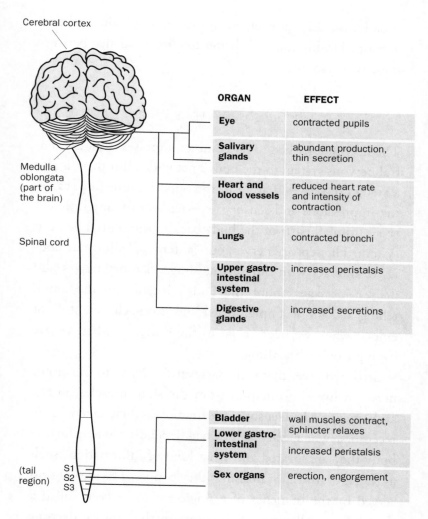

FIGURE 4.5   The parasympathetic nervous system. (Note that most of the functions have their opposite in the sympathetic nervous system.)

situation but are more active in situations of calm and connection. Health and well-being require a balance between
these two systems.

The Sensory Nervous System

The nerves described so far conduct impulses from the central nervous system to the body's networks. But there is also
a system of nerves that go in the opposite direction, carry-
ing impressions and sensory experiences of many different
types from all parts of the body back to the central nervous
system. The sensory nerves, our "antennas," allow our bodies to interact with our surroundings. Sensory nerves also
deliver messages about the body's interior to the brain,
telling us, for example, when our stomachs are full or
empty, when we need to go to the toilet, or when we are
having trouble breathing.

Sensory nerves that run "backward" relative to the motor
nerves deliver information from the skin, muscles, joints,
and sinews. This sensory information is first taken in by
receptors, which vary somewhat depending where in the
body they are located and what kind of information (such
as touch, warmth, or pressure) they convey. The area of skin
served by the branches of a single spinal nerve is called a
dermatome. All types of receptors in the sensory nervous
system have the same function: to carry sensations from one
part of the body via the nerves to the central nervous system.

Several types of receptors are activated by mechanical stimulation. Because of this, we can feel when we bend or stretch a joint, and we can experience someone else's touch. The skin's receptors have the ability to register and respond to different types of touch and pressure, as well as different temperatures, allowing us to distinguish between a light stroking and a rougher touch, a warm hand and a cold one.

The speed at which the impulses from these receptors are transported through the ingoing nerves depends on the thickness of the nerve fibers and is correlated in part with what type of sensory information is being conveyed. When you experience a pleasant touch, certain types of nerves take the information to the brain; but when you feel discomfort and pain, other types convey that information. Touch in general and acute pain are conveyed by fast-conducting thick fibers, and pain of a more chronic nature is carried more slowly in thin nerves. A special type of thin and slow-conducting nerve fiber has recently been discovered, one that is activated by a regular light touch and conveys pleasant sensations.

All sensory information passes through the spinal cord to areas higher up in the central nervous system. Eventually, the messages reach the thalamus, an important location in the brain for processing sensations, and finally arrive at the sensory area in the cerebral cortex. Then, for the first time, the information is revealed to us, and we can be conscious of the touch or the pain that the receptors at the other end of the sensory nerves responded to a moment before.

When the sensory information reaches the cerebral cortex, we can respond in many different ways. We can have an immediate reaction, such as a startled movement. We can return a caress or move away to avoid further pain—or we can simply store the information in memory with the option of responding at some later time.

But as this sensory information is following its fast track along thick fibers to the higher parts of the brain, it can also reach the older parts of the brain and produce effects of which we are unaware. The activation of thin, slow-conducting nerve fibers, especially, causes reactions in the brain's evolutionarily older parts at the lower brain level. Light touch or chronic pain, which are conveyed by such nerves, can therefore produce physiological effects without our being aware of them; this process can affect bodily processes associated with calm and connection, as when pleasant touch lowers levels of stress hormones and blood pressure. The physiology behind this effect of touch will be explained later in the book.

Sensory nerves also connect the autonomic nervous system to the central nervous system. One such sensory nerve is the vagus nerve, which conveys information from the abdominal organs, the heart, and the lungs. Ninety percent of the nerve fibers in the vagus nerve transport sensory information to the brain from these organs.

Information about the digestive system (fullness, percentage of acidity, and more) goes to the brain via the vagus nerve. Information about the degree of lung inflation and the condition of the heart muscle and blood vessels also

THE SENSORY NERVOUS SYSTEM

1. Transmits sensations from the body to the central nervous system.

2. Includes nerves from the skin, muscles, joints, and sinews, most often leading from the spinal cord to the brain.

3. Also includes nerves that, via the autonomic nervous system (the vagal nerves), convey information from abdominal organs, heart, and lungs, as well as from the skin on the front of the body without passing the spinal cord.

Information from the sensory organs is received by special nerves in the brain. Brain nerves can consist of motor, sensory, voluntary, and/or autonomic nerve fibers.

reaches the brain via the autonomic nervous system. This input is used by the outgoing nerves and hormones that regulate these organs. Bodily pain is also conveyed via the autonomic nervous system's ingoing sensory fibers. Since pain information can often be imprecise, it is sometimes difficult for a doctor to make a correct diagnosis of, for example, appendicitis, when it is hard to tell exactly where the pain is located.

Curiously, an additional group of sensory nerves follow the vagus branch. These are sensory nerves from the uterus and mammary glands, as well as probably from the skin on the chest. Similar to the vagal sensory nerves from the inner organs such as the stomach, these nerves do not convey their messages through the spinal cord but reach other low parts of the central nervous system directly. They probably do not convey precise information about the location of touch, but more likely influence the deeper parts of the brain that deal with feelings and physiological reactions.

Nerves in the Head

Last but not least are the nerve connections in the head, where we have our major sensory organs for sight, taste, smell, hearing, and balance. These organs, along with our facial muscles, enable us to orient ourselves to our surroundings. There are fundamentally twelve major nerve branches between the brain and the head, both motor (outgoing and controlling) and sensory (incoming and feeling).

An abundance of autonomic nerve fibers, both sensory and motor, control involuntary responses in the head. When, for example, the pupil changes size or the ear separates out meaningful sounds from background noise, it is because the autonomic nerve impulses in the sight or hearing nerves are fine-tuning the functioning of those sensory organs.

We react to more than we are consciously aware of. Besides the familiar organ of smell in the nose, there is also in the nasal passage a less well-known sensory mechanism called the vomero-nasal organ. Through it, we register the presence of pheromones, biochemicals that have odors we do not consciously perceive but which play an important role in communication and interpersonal contacts, especially sexual attraction. Pheromones cause physiological reactions without first passing their information through our conscious thought processes.

Besides orienting us to our surroundings, information from our sense organs can also have a strong emotional impact on us. When we hear sirens or other sounds that we associate with danger, we may experience fear and a pounding heart. The pitch of a voice can make us react with interest or with aversion, depending on whether we interpret the sound as friendly or aggressive. A person's expression, from the many variations of a smile to a sternly wrinkled brow, can also evoke in us widely different feelings.

The skin of the face, like the skin of the hands, is extremely sensitive. Sensory receptors there are close together, and the area of the cerebral cortex that receives information from the face and hands is also large in proportion to the amount of body surface they take up. We know that much communication occurs between people through body language rather than words.

Although we can control certain facial muscles voluntarily, many of our expressions materialize outside our voluntary control, as when we unintentionally blush or flash a smile to try to put an insecure companion at ease. A good interpreter of body language can differentiate between false

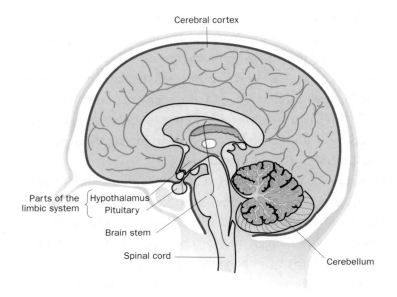

FIGURE 4.6   The location of the hypothalamus and the pituitary in the brain.

and sincere smiles; this is because a smile that involves only the mouth can be put on at will, but a smile that also involves the small muscles around the eyes conveys the message that true feeling exists.

The Hypothalamus and the Pituitary

Two important brain centers, the hypothalamus and the pituitary, are especially significant to our understanding of oxytocin and the calm and connection system.

A significant number of the body's autonomic functions are controlled from the hypothalamus. To a large degree, this part of the brain regulates the functioning of internal organs, such as the working of the heart muscle, the circulation of the blood, the activities of digestion, and secretions from various glands.

The hypothalamus has two ways to reach out to these organs: through the sympathetic and the parasympathetic parts of the autonomic nervous system. The hypothalamus also operates by influencing the hormonal control system found in the pituitary gland. In this way, the hypothalamus and the body communicate through autonomic nerve impulses and hormones secreted into the bloodstream.

Many of the body's autonomic activities are also connected with strong feelings. If you are frightened, your heart begins to beat more rapidly. Your feeling—in this case, fear—is experienced in part because of activity in the amygdala, an almond-shaped cell group in the brain located in the anterior extremity of the temporal lobe, which is linked to emotional reactions and emotional memories. Nerve pathways going in both directions connect the areas in the hypothalamus that control bodily functions with the areas in the amygdala that are related to emotions. In this way, feelings and simultaneous physical reactions are strongly linked, no matter which system is activated first.

When the hypothalamus generates hormonal activity, the hormones are supplied to various organs in the body via the pituitary. This gland has two parts, a frontal lobe

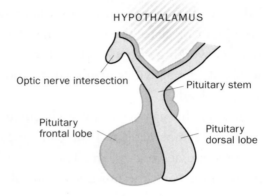

FIGURE 4.7   The pituitary's frontal and dorsal lobes.

and a dorsal lobe. Special cells in the frontal lobe produce such well-known hormones as growth hormone; the milk-producing hormone prolactin; the hormones that in turn stimulate creation of the stress hormone cortisol; the thyroid-stimulating hormone; and sex hormones, which stimulate the ovaries and testicles. These hormones spread throughout the body in the bloodstream, influencing a large number of organs. It is the hypothalamus, however, that ultimately controls all these hormonal signals through an intricate feedback system.

A Dual Role

While the hormones named above are formed in as well as secreted from the pituitary's frontal lobe, oxytocin and vaso-

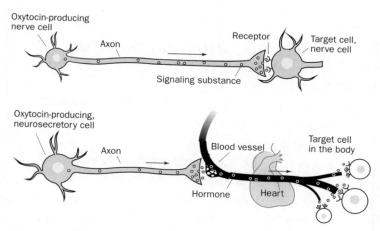

FIGURE 4.8 Oxytocin functions both as a signaling substance in the nerve pathways and as a hormone in the blood. *Above:* Oxytocin as a signaling substance influences the target cell directly via receptors. *Below:* Oxytocin as a hormone influences the target cell via transport in the bloodstream.

pressin are instead created in two parts of the hypothalamus, the supraoptic nucleus and the paraventricular nucleus. From there they are transported to the pituitary's dorsal lobe and released into the blood to be delivered to their respective target organs.

Oxytocin and vasopressin are not only released into the bloodstream as hormones via the pituitary gland but also delivered directly from the hypothalamus to the nervous system through long nerve fibers. In this way, the two biochemicals behave like signaling substances in many places in the brain and spinal cord. They influence, for example, the areas of the brain that in turn direct the activity of the autonomic nervous system.

THE HYPOTHALAMUS AND THE PITUITARY

The hypothalamus
- controls involuntary functions in the internal organs, such as the heart, blood vessels, gastrointestinal system, and glands;
- controls via the autonomic nervous system as well as via hormones; and
- produces oxytocin and vasopressin in its supraoptic nucleus (for transport to the pituitary) and in its paraventricular nucleus (for transport to the pituitary and for direct release in the nervous system).

The pituitary
- consists of a frontal lobe and a dorsal lobe;
- carries hormonal information from the hypothalamus to different organs; and
- from the dorsal lobe secretes oxytocin and vasopressin into the blood.

Thus oxytocin and vasopressin function in two parallel ways, as hormones in the bloodstream and as signaling substances in the central nervous system. For example, vasopressin causes increased blood pressure in part because its localized effect as a blood-borne hormone causes the musculature in the blood vessels to contract, and in part because its influence as a signaling substance increases the activity of the sympathetic nervous system, which in turn raises the blood pressure.

Whether the body's chemical messengers are transmitted from nerve endings or reach their target organs directly via the blood, special receptors are needed to produce an effect. These receptors, located on or inside the cells, are ingeniously adapted to react only to a certain substance, or at least only to closely related substances. (See Figure 4.8.)

The task both of hormones and of nerves is to convey information and coordinate activity in the body. The two systems function in different but complementary ways. Hormones in general travel throughout the body via the bloodstream, but their activity is regulated by the presence or absence of receptors in various organs or parts of the body. Individual nerves, in contrast, reach only a limited area where they deliver signaling substances that cause specific localized effects. As we will see, this dual system for transmitting biochemical information increases the powerful effects of oxytocin throughout the body.

In the next chapter, we'll explore what kind of substance oxytocin actually is and how it interacts with other substances in the body.

5

How Oxytocin Works

Research into hormones has advanced significantly in recent decades. Today, we recognize two types. The first group, called *steroids,* is composed of fats related to cholesterol. These hormones act by passing through the cell wall and affecting the cell nucleus. The other group of hormones is called *peptides*, or *polypeptides*, which are small proteins consisting of a combination of amino acids. Peptides generally operate differently from steroids, not by entering the cell itself but by activating receptors on the outer surface of the cell membrane. Oxytocin and vasopressin belong to the peptide hormone group.

Oxytocin exists in identical composition in all species of mammals, but vasopressin shows slight variations in molecular structure. As mentioned in the previous chapter, both substances are created in the supraoptic and paraventricular nuclei of the hypothalamus. Nerve fibers run from these cell groups to the pituitary gland, located lower in the

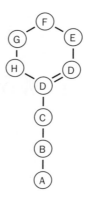

FIGURE 5.1   The oxytocin molecule is composed of nine amino acids, A–H.

brain, from which point the hormones are released into the circulatory system. Oxytocin and vasopressin also operate as signaling substances in the nervous system, since nerve fibers from the paraventricular cell group connect in a fan-like pattern with many other parts of the brain.

Oxytocin and vasopressin are produced in the supraoptic and paraventricular nuclei by two types of cells: large and small. The large cells send their oxytocin to the pituitary gland; the small cells reach out to other parts of the brain through their axons.

Singing in Unison

The cells that produce oxytocin have an interesting characteristic. As I described earlier, an electric current passes through a nerve cell when it is activated. In the oxytocin-pro-

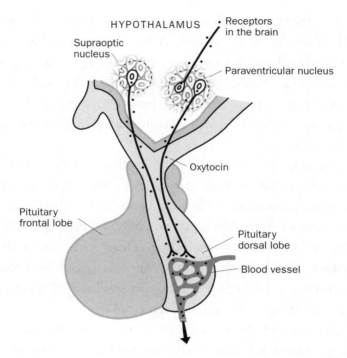

FIGURE 5.2   Oxytocin signals go out through nerve fibers from the hypothalamus to the dorsal lobe of the pituitary gland and to receptors in the brain.

ducing cells, these electric impulses do not come one by one, but in a cluster. If these cells are powerfully stimulated, as in nursing, the electrical activity becomes coordinated. Cells that normally lie between oxytocin-producing cells as a sort of insulation disappear, and all the oxytocin-producing cells begin to act in concert. It is in part because the cells behave in this way that we see such great rises in oxytocin levels in the blood of nursing women.

The coordination that occurs with oxytocin-producing cells is unique in physiology. As we look more closely at oxytocin's effects, we discover, interestingly enough, that *coordination,* whether of cells, effects, or individuals, is a marker for oxytocin and something that distinguishes it from many other substances in the bodies of humans and other mammals.

The areas of the brain that are influenced by oxytocin and vasopressin through nerves from the hypothalamus include areas close to the hypothalamus and the brain stem, sites connected with the regulation of blood pressure, pulse, alertness, movement, and feeling. These same nerves also connect with locations in the brain and spinal cord that control the activity of the autonomic nervous system as well as the sensation of pain. (See Figure 5.3.)

This intricate branching out of nerve fibers from the hypothalamus makes it possible for the body to coordinate many different physiological functions and activities, using both oxytocin and vasopressin as messengers.

The oxytocin that leaves through the bloodstream as a hormone and the oxytocin that travels by way of the nerves as a signaling substance can be coordinated in certain situations. They are separated to a degree by something called the "blood-brain barrier"; this barrier consists of tightly packed cells in the blood vessels of the brain that prevent substances from leaking into the brain tissue. This mechanism is a sort of security system to protect the brain against dangerous toxins, but it also keeps out potentially helpful substances such as blood-borne oxytocin. From this, we can conclude that oxytocin found in the brain originates in the oxytocin-producing cells located there.

Oxytocin Receptors

Whether transported in the blood or sending signals through nerves, oxytocin works in the body through special receptors where the biochemical can "plug in." There are many different types of such receptors in the body, and a given substance can connect to several types. In that way, a single hormone can have various functions.

Three different types of receptors for vasopressin have been found. They are related to, among other things, blood pressure and kidney function. It is likely that oxytocin also works through several different sorts of receptors, but so far only one has been identified: the one that connects oxytocin with the contracting mechanism of the uterus. We know that this type of receptor is also found in other parts of the body, for example, in the brain.

One way of researching oxytocin receptors has been to use an oxytocin antagonist (antidote) to block oxytocin's physiological effects by connecting with the receptors first so that they are not accessible to the oxytocin. Because some of oxytocin's effects have nevertheless appeared when this antidote has been used, researchers believe there must be several types of oxytocin receptors, even if they cannot yet identify them. The existence of such undiscovered receptors

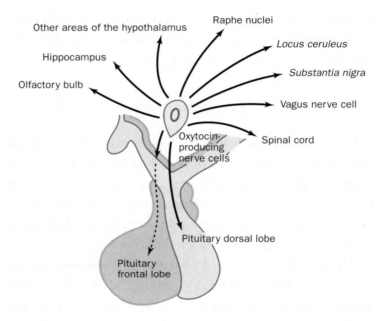

FIGURE 5.3   Oxytocin-producing nerve cells.

would explain why some of the places to which oxytocin nerves run have no known oxytocin receptors. We can hope that research will soon identify the missing receptors.

How Oxytocin Is Controlled

The release of oxytocin is controlled primarily by nerves that run to the paraventricular nucleus of the brain and carry information both from the outside world (for example, via the skin) and from inside the body (for example, the uterus and the intestines). Often, several nerve connections are made before the final nerve reaches the paraventricular nucleus where oxytocin is produced.

Oxytocin production can also be influenced by nerves from other areas inside the brain, for example, the olfactory bulb, various locations in the cerebral cortex, or older and lower parts of the brain such as the brain stem. These nerves can either increase or reduce the secretion of oxytocin.

Animal experiments have shown that oxytocin in certain situations can have a stronger effect in females than in males, even though the distribution of oxytocin-producing cells and the circulation of the substance in the bloodstream are more or less similar for both sexes. The female sex hormone estrogen can also activate the oxytocin system by increasing the production of oxytocin. Estrogen has recently been found to act on two different receptors, the alpha and the beta type. The beta type seems to be linked to oxytocin release. During childbirth and nursing, oxytocin is released by activation of sensory nerves.

Nerves communicate, as mentioned before, through chemical messengers, the so-called signaling substances or neurotransmitters. Many such messengers carry information to the hypothalamus and its centers where oxytocin is produced. Some of these messages produce an increase in oxytocin; others inhibit its release. For example, the amino acids glutamate and GABA (y-aminobutyric acid) respectively increase and inhibit oxytocin secretion. Enkephalin, beta-endorphin, and dynorphin block its production; cholecystokinin (CCK) and vasoactive intestinal polypeptide (VIP) stimulate its release.

Mono-amines such as serotonin, dopamine, and noradrenaline are altered amino acids that operate as important signaling substances. Neurons that contain serotonin stimulate the release of oxytocin. This may explain in part why selective serotonin reuptake inhibitors (SSRIs)—such as Prozac—that increase the serotonin level can influence a person's state of mind and anxiety level. By raising the serotonin level, these drugs indirectly increase the oxytocin level. (The pervasive role of oxytocin in the action of many sedatives and antidepressants is discussed in Chapter 16.) Dopamine, which plays an important role in controlling movements and concentration, is also of crucial importance for the body's own internal reward systems. Dopamine also causes a rise in the oxytocin level.

The stress hormone noradrenaline has a more paradoxical effect. A large noradrenaline system in the brain emanates from a cell group with the vivid name *locus ceruleus,* literally "blue place." This system, which normally has an activating effect on alertness and aggression, is also an important target for oxytocin's effect in the brain. Like serotonin and dopamine, noradrenaline has a stimulating effect on the release of oxytocin.

In addition, there is a peculiarity in the control of oxytocin. Most hormones tend to shut off their own production with the help of a thermostat-like feedback system. To maintain balance, hormones also operate as signaling substances to oppose their own secretion when their level exceeds a certain amount. But oxytocin does the opposite. It stimulates its own production to a certain level by acti-

OXYTOCIN IN THE BODY

1. Oxytocin and vasopressin are peptides, closely related in chemical composition. They are found practically unchanged in all species of mammals.
2. Oxytocin and vasopressin are produced in the supraoptic and paraventricular nuclei of the hypothalamus.
3. Oxytocin is both a hormone, which acts in the body through the bloodstream, and a signaling substance in the nervous system.
4. Certain endogenous substances (made within the body) such as GABA, and opiates such as enkephalin, beta-endorphin, and dynorphin, inhibit the release of oxytocin.
5. Other substances, such as glutamate, CCK, VIP, serotonin, dopamine, noradrenaline, and oxytocin itself, stimulate the release of oxytocin.
6. The female sex hormone estrogen can increase the number of oxytocin receptors and stimulate the production of oxytocin.
7. Oxytocin influences activity in other receptors and signaling systems.

vating oxytocin receptors on the oxytocin-producing cells, and these newly activated receptors stimulate the cells to produce more oxytocin.

The oxytocin-containing nerve cells branch out in a fan-like network, and, as we have said, the substance likely has not one but several types of receptors. These nerves and receptors together constitute a complex system that influences various physiological activities. Oxytocin is seldom the last link in the chain but functions by altering or modulating the activities in other major systems. Simultaneously, these systems work in a feedback loop to influence oxytocin production. Oxytocin can also have entirely different types of localized effects in body tissues. New discoveries are showing that oxytocin is produced in many different places, including the ovaries and testicles, as well as the heart and the walls of blood vessels. We do not yet know what this locally produced oxytocin does, but it assuredly strengthens the effects of the blood-borne oxytocin. In the rest of the book, we will explore these wide-ranging and often astonishing effects.

PART THREE ❧

Oxytocin's Effects

~ 6

Effects of Oxytocin Injections

Oxytocin is with us throughout our lives. When you were born, oxytocin helped expel you from your mother's womb and then made it possible for her to nurse you. As a small child, you enjoyed your mother's and father's loving touch because it released oxytocin in your body. As an adult, you experience the effects of oxytocin when you enjoy good food, or a massage, or an intimate interlude with your romantic partner. Oxytocin is active in all these situations, and more.

Many of the effects of oxytocin described in this book have been demonstrated in research with animals. Researchers have observed not only changes in animals' behavior but also various measurable physiological changes in their bodies. Most of these effects have also been confirmed in humans, not as a result of experimental doses of oxytocin but by observation of changes that occur in connection with the natural release of the substance.

Less Fearful, More Sociable and Nurturing

Oxytocin functions as a "turbo-booster" for several types of normal behavior in rats. Greater amounts of the substance cause the effects to be achieved more quickly.

Rats that receive low doses of oxytocin become less fearful and more curious. They are more likely to dare to leave the safety of the nest and explore unfamiliar surroundings. Oxytocin has a clear antianxiety effect.

When given oxytocin, groups of rats of the same sex become more gregarious and less afraid of contact. As aggression in the group decreases noticeably, friendly socializing replaces it. Rather than avoid each other, the rats prefer to sit near each other. This closeness leads in its turn to the release of still more oxytocin. (Later we will see how touch and bodily contact play a big role in the release of oxytocin.)

It is interesting that vasopressin, oxytocin's "sister" substance, which differs by only two amino acids, also makes rats unafraid, but in an entirely different manner. Vasopressin instills courage by making the individual feel aggressive and fearless. The rat, male or female, is prepared to attack, mark territory, and vigorously defend itself. Oxytocin instead fosters courage by diminishing the feeling of danger and conveying the sense that there is less to be afraid of. Animal studies appear to show that oxytocin has a special ability to make animals "nice." Physiologically, therefore, a substance related to strength and readiness (vasopressin) is a close relative to one that produces friendliness and caring (oxytocin). They function in different ways, and we need them both. As the popular Swedish fictional character Pippi Longstocking says, "The one who is powerfully strong must also be powerfully nice."

Sexual behavior is also stimulated by oxytocin. Oxytocin injections have been shown to accelerate mating, perhaps by reducing fear. Mating in turn leads to the release of oxytocin in both females and males. This release is believed to play a role in, among other things, the transport of the egg and sperm. (Oxytocin and human sexuality are discussed in Chapter 11.)

A striking example of behavior influenced by oxytocin is the interaction between a mother and her young. Rats are timid animals, and normally a female rat is afraid of strangers, including young rats not her own. But when female rats are treated in advance with the female sex hormone estrogen and then given an injection of oxytocin, they begin to exhibit maternal behavior even if they have not produced offspring. In rat terms, this means that they build a nest, carry to it any young in the vicinity, lick and clean them, and defend them against strange rats. Even though these females have no milk, they lie down as though preparing to nurse.

When females actually do have babies, the release of oxytocin is stimulated in the mother during birth and suckling. As we have seen, oxytocin stimulates the uterus to contract and expel the newborn, and it causes the muscles surrounding the milk ducts to contract and expel breast milk. (More about nursing in Chapter 8.) Nursing rats have been

. to lose their natural fear and to keep right on about their maternal business even in the presence of noise and intense light.

Enhanced Social Memory

Memory and learning are complicated processes that involve many different parts of the brain. When someone makes an indelible impression on us, it may be because we are afraid of that person, but we also may have positive reactions to that person because we met him or her under the influence of oxytocin's nectar, at a time when we felt really good and open to our surroundings.

Oxytocin is thought to have a positive effect on what we call social memory, which, like fear and sociability, is processed to a large extent in the amygdala (discussed in Chapter 4). One example is the ability to recognize someone we have met before, something that animals obviously can also learn. This recognition is speeded up in animals treated with oxytocin. Oxytocin can also hasten the development of "acquaintanceship" in animals, so that they prefer certain individuals over others. A special variant of this ability to recognize acquaintances is bonding or attachment, which happens when, for example, a mother learns to recognize and prefer her own young over others. The mother and her offspring may come to know and bond with each other more quickly because the level of oxytocin is so high in connection with birthing.

In one experiment, the oxytocin effect led a female vole to prefer a particular male of her species. If she was given an injection of oxytocin when she had a certain male in front of her, she not only recognized that animal from then on but also chose him in preference to others. Oxytocin is physiology's "forget-me-not" that makes recognition and bonding reverberate in the nerves' pathways. We see this in humans as well. We can also become unforgettable for each other if oxytocin is released when we come together. Someone we have been very close to, in a love relationship, for example, will always be special to us.

Increased Calm and Less Pain

We have seen that small amounts of oxytocin reduce anxiety and increase curiosity, but larger amounts produce an entirely different effect. A cow will stand still, look drowsy, and sometimes start to ruminate. Rats become calmer, move around less, and may even draw aside to rest or sleep. These effects—in particular reduced curiosity—become more apparent after several oxytocin injections, and they persist long after the last dose has been given.

Another effect in oxytocin's wide sphere of influence is its ability to alleviate pain. Oxytocin sends signals along nerve fibers from their site of origin in the hypothalamus to several areas in the nervous system that relate to the sensation of pain. After oxytocin injections, a rat takes longer to pull its paw away from a hot surface or to flick its tail out of water that is too hot. This behavior can be interpreted as evidence of oxytocin's ability to reduce the sensation of pain. It is probably not that the pain impulse from the paw is registered as weaker, but instead that the reaction to the message of pain diminishes.

Just as the antianxiety effect becomes stronger and longer-lasting after repeated injections, the threshold for reaction to pain increases after multiple oxytocin treatments. The rats' reaction to the heat stimuli described above can remain diminished even a week after the last oxytocin injection.

Improved Learning Ability

Have you ever tried to learn something new or understand something complicated when you are under stress and pressed for time? Anyone who has been in that situation has known frustration. Your concentration works better if you have had a chance to calm down, either by being left in peace for a while or by having enough time for what you are doing. Since oxytocin reduces stress, it can improve opportunities for learning.

Oxytocin has had an undeservedly bad reputation with regard to memory. For example, some people have claimed that women forget the pangs of childbirth because their oxytocin level is so high at that time. In some animal studies, oxytocin injections have led to worse memory. In tests of rat learning, such as navigating a maze, oxytocin has had a short-term negative effect on memory functions. Vasopressin has had the opposite effect, facilitating learning. It is possible that this effect is caused by the vasopressin, which makes the animals more alert, and that this increased wakefulness lies behind the improvement in memory.

I've observed, however, that the effect of oxytocin is most often precisely the opposite; it improves learning ability, especially if injections of the substance are repeated several times. By chance, my colleagues and I discovered that a special type of laboratory rat has a difficult time learning to avoid an unpleasant situation, for example, a weak electric shock. Ordinary rats learned very quickly to avoid this negative stimulus. But after five oxytocin injections, the animals that at first had difficulty learning became as clever as the normal rats at avoiding the shock. Even several days after the end of the oxytocin injections, the usually "dumb" rats retained their improved memory. This effect appears to have little direct connection with the rats' intelligence or memory functions, but is a result of the calming effect of oxytocin described above.

We all know it's difficult to learn something if one is extremely drowsy. But it is equally difficult if we try to learn something new while anxious and stressed. It's best to be just alert and just relaxed enough. When a friend advises you to calm down and take it easy when everything is piling up around you, difficult as that may seem, it is good advice for several reasons. When you achieve a better balance internally between stress hormones and calm and connection hormones, you will not only feel better but also probably comprehend the situation better and find more adaptive solutions.

In fact, the rats that were considered "dumb" but later showed improvements in learning after oxytocin treatment were also (before the oxytocin injections) easier to disturb and had higher levels of the stress hormone cortisol than rats with ordinary learning abilities; after the injections, however, the symptoms of stress in the "dumb" rats normalized. This is a provocative finding, since we can observe that people who are stressed and depressed also generally have difficulties with learning.

The long-term effects of oxytocin cannot depend on the direct influence of the substance, since it disappears very quickly from the blood. The reason why the effects can last for many days after the last injection probably has to do with oxytocin's ability to influence the operation of other signaling substances in a long-lasting way. (More about that in the next chapter.)

Effects on Blood Pressure

Just as we can measure indications of oxytocin's mildly activating and calming effects on behavior, we can also observe other ways that it produces activity and relaxation. Oxytocin can, for example, raise and lower the pulse rate and blood pressure. Which effect is produced depends on the situation, the animal's hormone levels, and the type of animal used in the research.

EFFECTS OF OXYTOCIN INJECTIONS ON BEHAVIOR

The following changes in behavior have been observed in animals (especially rats) after oxytocin injections:
- a rapid development of maternal behavior (even in females who have never had babies);
- stimulated and facilitated mating;
- more social contact between individuals;
- less anxiety, increased boldness and curiosity (with low doses of oxytocin);
- a·calming, even sleep-inducing effect (with high doses of oxytocin);
- a diminished sensation of pain (more powerful and long-lasting alleviation with repeated injections); and
- facilitated learning, even in individuals with learning difficulties.

In apes and humans, oxytocin appears to lower only pulse and blood pressure. The effects are produced by influencing the sympathetic and parasympathetic nerves, either directly or through connections higher up in the brain. As we saw, the paraventricular cell group in the hypothalamus is one of the locations in the brain where oxytocin is produced. When this part of the brain was electrically stimulated, the animals' blood pressure went down. This effect probably occurs because the electrical current causes the release of oxytocin into the areas of the brain where blood pressure is controlled.

Oxytocin's effect is gradual. When single injections are given, pulse rate and blood pressure increase temporarily, then sink slowly to a level lower than they were before the injection. If we administer oxytocin several times, blood pressure is significantly lowered, an effect that lasts longer than the result produced by a single injection.

Even though oxytocin is not solely a female hormone, its effects in females are more pronounced. If oxytocin is given to female animals five days in a row, the lowered blood pressure lasts for three weeks. In male animals, the effect on blood pressure is the same, but lasts only half as long. The reason for this difference is the female sex hormone estrogen, which, as we saw, reinforces the influence of oxytocin and produces the longer-lasting effect in females. Female rats without ovaries, like males, lack this reinforcement, and accordingly the lowered blood pressure does not last as long with them. However, in both these females and the males, the effect lasts for three weeks if they receive twice as many injections. Females without ovaries and males must therefore have twice the amount of oxytocin to achieve the same effect produced in females with normal estrogen levels.

Balancing Body Temperature

Each individual, human or nonhuman, must be able to control body temperature. In humans, this is done through sweating and shivering. In rats, the tail is the most important way to regulate temperature. A red tail means that the blood vessels are dilated, and energy in the form of body heat is escaping. But when the blood vessels in the tail contract, less heat escapes and the rat conserves energy.

Oxytocin can influence body temperature in part by lowering the temperature of the tail in rats and allowing the rat to conserve energy. The heat is redistributed so that the tail becomes cold, but other parts of the body become warmer. Other research supports this view of oxytocin as a sort of thermostat that does not keep the temperature constant but instead shifts the warmth from one part of the body to another.

In a suckling mother rat, the blood vessels on the frontal side are dilated by oxytocin. This means that the female can warm her small offspring while they nurse. The same phenomenon appears also in nursing women, as well as with fathers who are holding their babies. These blood vessels also dilate in both men and women during sexual activity. In all these situations we see warm chests and rosy cheeks. Oxytocin is the reason.

Regulating Digestion

Oxytocin plays yet another important role in the process of converting food and drink in the body. An interesting aspect of oxytocin's role in digestion is that it differs according to whether an animal is full or hungry. A sort of intelligence applies to oxytocin's way of working, because its effects vary to promote the optimal outcome in each situation.

Animals receiving oxytocin lose their appetites for several hours. But over a longer period, oxytocin injections produce increased appetite, especially in females and in connection with nursing. Over time, the digestive process works more effectively, in part because oxytocin stimulates the secretion of gastric juices and the release of digestive hormones such as gastrin, cholecystokinin, somatostatin, and insulin. The last three also help promote the storage of nourishment in the body.

Oxytocin can cause two entirely different response patterns, depending on the situation. Animals with food in their stomachs react with increased digestive activity and storage of nutrition. But if they are hungry—their stomachs empty—they have a reaction that inhibits the digestive process. Oxytocin produces both these effects by influencing the activity in the part of the parasympathetic nervous system (the vagus nerve) that controls the functioning of the intestines. (Chapter 14 will show other examples of nature's ingenious method for optimal adaptation to each situation.)

Regulating Fluid Levels

Another balancing act accomplished by oxytocin is its effect on fluid levels in the body. Oxytocin works with its partner hormone, vasopressin, to maintain the body's fluid balance by either expelling water, especially in the form of urine, or promoting the storage of bodily fluids. Oxytocin and vasopressin have entirely opposite effects on fluid levels.

Oxytocin, not surprisingly, is responsible for the first function. It stimulates the extraction of sodium by the kidneys and promotes urination. Animals receiving oxytocin become less enthusiastic about eating salt; the result is a lowering of the body's sodium content and a reduction in the retention of water.

As for conserving bodily fluids, an increase in the stress hormones vasopressin and corticotropin releasing factor (CRF) produces an increased desire for salt. Vasopressin leads also to decreased urine production and the retention of salt and fluid. At the same time, it contracts the blood vessels, producing higher blood pressure. We need to conserve fluids if our situation appears dangerous and we are at risk of wounds that would cause the loss of blood and other body fluids. Vasopressin and CRF accomplish this.

Growth and Healing of Wounds

Oxytocin stimulates growth, not only by promoting the development of the animal as a whole but also by accelerating the healing of wounds. Oxytocin injections make sores on a rat's back heal more quickly than they would otherwise. They also heal and rejuvenate mucous membranes, and produce anti-inflammatory reactions.

Effects on Other Hormones

As we saw, both oxytocin and vasopressin are produced in the hypothalamus and transported to the pituitary gland's

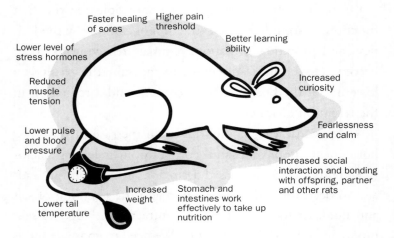

FIGURE 6.1   Effects of oxytocin injections in rats.

dorsal lobe, from which they are released into the blood-stream. The pituitary's frontal lobe secretes several other hormones, but these are regulated in a manner different from that of the dorsal lobe hormones. Special control substances created in the hypothalamus are conducted through a localized circulation system to the pituitary's frontal lobe, where they cause the release of the other hormones into the bloodstream.

Certain nerves release oxytocin into the blood vessels that connect with the pituitary's frontal lobe. In this way, oxytocin stimulates the pituitary's release of, for example, prolactin, growth hormone (GH), and adrenocorticotropic hormone (ACTH). The increased levels of these hormones produce various effects. Prolactin, for example, stimulates the production of milk in suckling females and nursing

PHYSIOLOGICAL EFFECTS OF OXYTOCIN INJECTIONS

1. Short-term activating effect in the form of higher blood pressure, pulse, and levels of stress hormones (with single injection)
2. Lower blood pressure, pulse, and levels of stress hormones (with repeated injections) over a longer period
3. Longer-lasting effects in females with estrogen
4. Raised body temperature in rats (and other animals, including humans), especially on the frontal side, but lower temperature in the tail
5. Reduced muscle tension
6. Temporarily reduced appetite; but with repeated injections, increased appetite over the longer term
7. Stimulated digestion when the stomach is full, inhibited when empty
8. Increased urination, in part by causing the body to excrete more salt and in part by reducing the desire for salt, which causes the body to retain less water
9. Faster-healing wounds, reduced inflammation

mothers. Growth hormone stimulates the body's growth, and ACTH directs the production of the stress hormone cortisol by the adrenal gland.

The effect of oxytocin on ACTH and corticosterone is, however, much more complicated. As we saw with respect to blood pressure, oxytocin can initially give rise to a short-term increase in ACTH and thereby in the level of corticosterone, at least in rats. But as before, this stimulating effect of oxytocin is short-lived. After a brief time, this increase switches over to its opposite, and the level drops. With repeated treatments, a long-term lowering of corticosterone is achieved. This effect occurs because the entire control system is influenced. Production of the control substance ACTH in the hypothalamus drops, as does the production of corticosterone in the adrenal gland. As a result, the regulating system that attempts to keep the level constant becomes less sensitive. Low cortisol levels, in turn, contribute to a state of calm, quiet, and well-being. The body's innate system of checks and balances is complex; oxytocin is constantly present and working in many different ways. The effects of this coordinated system are connected like the threads in a marvelous web.

7

The Oxytocin Tree

We have just seen oxytocin's effects on various physiological systems. Although these are remarkably varied, they all serve to further the need of animals, including humans, to grow and reproduce.

The Principle of Growth

The many different effects of oxytocin are like the branches of a large tree. Each arises from the basic principle (the trunk) associated with oxytocin, namely, the stimulation of growth.

Oxytocin stimulates growth through the transformation of food. Nourishment can be used in two ways in the body: Either it can be burned directly—that is, used as fuel for different bodily processes, such as generating heat or motion—or it can be stored in the tissues. Nutrition is

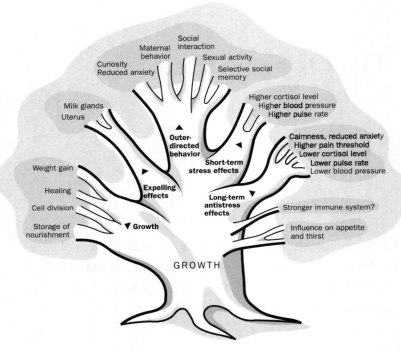

FIGURE 7.1   The oxytocin tree. Growth, the common denominator for most of oxytocin's effects, is the trunk of the oxytocin tree.

stored either by using caloric energy in the processes of healing and growing or by depositing the excess in fat cells.

Oxytocin's fundamental effect on the body's transformation of nourishment is that of enhancing growth. Under the effect of oxytocin, food is used to build up tissues. The various ways this happens can look vastly different when studied independently, but the basic principle is the same.

Growth Processes

A basic requirement for all growth is the incorporation of nourishment into the organism. Oxytocin meets this need in various ways, such as by stimulating the gastrointestinal hormones that increase the effectiveness of digestion and the storage of nutrients. But oxytocin also has the ability to stimulate the secretion of growth hormone from the pituitary gland directly. Through these different mechanisms, newborn rats administered oxytocin grow more quickly and also become larger adult animals. Female rats that receive oxytocin injections during pregnancy give birth to larger offspring, and female rats that receive it as adults gain more weight than untreated control animals.

Growth is probably also stimulated more indirectly, because wounds can heal twice as quickly with the application of oxytocin. This healing effect may result from the substance's ability to stimulate cell division, that is, to accelerate the creation of new cells. Oxytocin also appears to increase the production of "growth factors," substances in the blood that facilitate cell enlargement and cell division.

If oxytocin stimulates growth, it is no surprise that it is involved in reproduction. Oxytocin is found both in eggs and sperm, where it stimulates the release of eggs from the ovaries and the production of sperm in the testicles. Oxytocin injections can increase fertility and make the very first cell divisions after fertilization occur more quickly, causing the embryo to grow faster. Thus, from the earliest stages of life, oxytocin serves as our constant companion.

Living things need to store nourishment if they are to grow. Each cell division is preceded by an increase in size, caused by the storage of nutrients. It is impossible for a cell to divide if it does not first store nutrition; a cell line that could not do so would soon disappear. We might even think of pregnancy and birth as a gigantic form of cell division in which the original unit first increases in size and then divides in two. I like to think of the entire reproductive process as a complex variant of the fundamental oxytocin principle, which produces more life by first stimulating growth and then producing two beings by dividing the original one.

Expulsion

The second branch of the oxytocin tree involves the ability to expel. It includes the classic effect of oxytocin on the muscles of the uterus to expel the newborn, and on the muscles of the breast to expel milk during nursing. Thus it is possible for an organism first to divide in two—that is, to give birth to young—and then to transmit energy in the form of nourishment to the offspring. Oxytocin causes these effects by stimulating the coordinated muscles in the uterus and the breast, leading in turn to the expulsion of the child and later the milk.

Sociability, Curiosity, and Mating

A third branch of the tree consists of oxytocin's ability to stimulate behaviors of sociability and curiosity, such as daring to approach another individual, then interacting with, later recognizing, and perhaps choosing to be close to that other individual. This branch affects interactions in the form of maternal and social behavior.

Some level of sociability is necessary for reproduction, including sexual intercourse, nursing, and nurturing. When people become close, emotional connections form between them, sometimes short-term, often enduring. This dynamic applies to sexual relationships, parent-child relationships, and friendships. Giving of oneself is easier if there is a bond, an emotional connection. Relationships, whether sexual, nurturing, companionable, or even professional, are generally most productive and long-lasting if both parties are capable of reaching out and feeling close.

Oxytocin's anxiety-reducing effect probably also belongs on this branch: A low anxiety level is a prerequisite for humans and animals when they dare to approach strangers.

Connecting the Branches

As we saw earlier, vasopressin is involved in behavior marked by defensiveness, boundary setting, and aggression. Oxytocin instead produces behavior characterized by social interaction, friendliness, and curiosity. Rats that receive oxytocin prefer nearness to isolation. This proximity initiates a cycle of effects, since contact with others also releases oxytocin. From this dynamic arises bonding, or attachment between individuals. We see a similar effect in humans: between parent and child, between intimate partners, and in other significant relationships. All these kinds of behavior, and certain of their physiological components, are strengthened by oxytocin.

Two of oxytocin's major effects—growth and healing on the one hand, and social activity and competence on the other—may at first glance appear entirely different. But seen from a broad perspective, the two effects appear connected. As is especially clear with mammals, an individual who grows and "divides" benefits her offspring by staying close. After giving birth, the mother becomes not only sociable and nurturing but also bonded with her young. She feeds, warms, grooms, and nestles with her babies. This maternal bond, fed by oxytocin, is key to the continuation of the species. The bond connecting her young to each other is also important. Just as cells produced from the same tissue must not attack each other or the whole organism would be in danger, so offspring of the same individual must get along—and do, when oxytocin has its way.

Short-Term Activation

Yet another branch of the oxytocin tree involves certain short-term effects that contrast with the long-term ones. An oxytocin infusion temporarily raises the blood pressure and pulse rate and stimulates the secretion of stress hormones. These mildly activating effects complement those that promote growth. It is sometimes necessary, for example, to take the initiative in social interactions, not to mention how much energy it requires to go through childbirth! The mother's blood pressure must rise so that the baby's blood supply is protected during labor. Short-lived stress effects are also useful in responding to unfamiliar situations, when the unknown lies just around the corner. It can be risky, or even fatal, to relax before exploring new ground to discover whether it is entirely safe.

Long-Term Reduction of Stress

A large branch on the oxytocin tree consists of powerful and long-lasting antistress effects. As we saw, oxytocin has the ability to lower blood pressure and pulse rate, reduce the level of stress hormones, increase tolerance of pain, and promote learning and a feeling of calm. This effect generally appears only after a period of time because it is a sort of natural insurance system; only after a period of alertness is it safe for an animal or a human to settle down and relax.

These long-term effects produce a physiological condition that is the opposite of stress. Activity in the sympathetic nervous system is restricted, resulting in lower blood pressure and lower concentrations of stress hormones in the blood. At the same time, parts of the parasympathetic nervous system are activated to slow the heart rate and increase digestion and nutrition storage. These antistress effects have many functions, but their general outcome is to create the necessary preconditions for growth. Key growth-related activities such as the storage of nutrition, the healing of wounds, and reproduction itself are all enhanced when the individual is calm.

This long-term antistress effect is not caused by the direct working of oxytocin, since the substance disappears quickly from the blood. The effects probably last for many days or even weeks after the last oxytocin treatment because of the way oxytocin activates other physiological mechanisms.

Scientists still do not know exactly how the antistress effect is achieved physiologically, but research has uncovered some mechanisms that seem to be part of the explanation. The signaling substances noradrenaline and epinephrine, for example, are key components of the brain's stress management system. They produce their effect via special receptors in the nervous system, especially those called alpha- and beta-adrenoreceptors. With repeated oxytocin injections, activity increases in certain receptors called the alpha-2 adrenoreceptors, producing an antistress effect that is opposite to the effects of noradrenaline on the other adrenoreceptors. This means that, as a result of repeated oxytocin injections, noradrenaline's influence can in principle be switched over to its opposite, as though a ship's captain has given the order to reverse engines.

The long-lasting elevation of the pain threshold from repeated oxytocin injections produces a subgroup of antistress effects. An increased tolerance of pain seems to result from the increased secretion of endorphins, often called the body's own morphine, one of the most important mechanisms for pain reduction. The fact that oxytocin injections also affect the centers in the brain regulating cortisol secretion may be one reason that the body's level of this stress hormone drops.

Other smaller branches on the oxytocin tree represent oxytocin's effect on appetite and thirst, and its role in strengthening the immune system. These and many other branches will certainly become more fully leafed out as a result of future research.

Branches Swaying Together

Showing oxytocin's various effects as branches on a tree is an attempt to describe them individually, but naturally this works only in theory. In real life, these effects are kept in constant interactive motion by the influence of external factors and the body's own substances. Sometimes only one branch of the oxytocin tree sways visibly in the wind, but often there are several.

Research describing the isolated effects of oxytocin is based on animal experiments, but scientists can assume to some extent that certain of the situations producing calm and well-being in humans are also associated with the body's release of oxytocin. Animal research has helped identify these situations, and often relevant human oxytocin levels have been measured. Research has shown, for example, that oxytocin levels in the brain go up when we nurse, eat, make love, or, more generally, have physical contact with another individual.

Nursing is one activity that releases a large amount of oxytocin and sets in motion several branches of the oxytocin tree. When the mother's breast milk is expelled, both she and her child become peaceful and relaxed. In addition, their interaction is enhanced, and in both of them, the processes of digestion and nutritional storage become more effective.

With massage, to cite another example, the branch for social interaction is stirred when the anxiety level drops. People being massaged have noticed that they begin to see the individual giving the massage as a trustworthy person in whom they want to confide. (We'll return to the effects of massage in Chapter 13.)

The Need for Growth and Defense

We can view the two major systems discussed in this book—calm and connection, and fight or flight—as the more complex manifestations of two elemental physiological processes that can be observed even at the level of individual cells. The basic oxytocin principle is to take in nourishment, store it, and then divide while still remaining connected. The opposite principle is to convert nutrition into the energy of movement or heat and to close off the cell's permeability.

Both ways of handling energy, either storing up as potential or breaking down into action, are needed for every living thing, whether cell or complex organism, to thrive. The traditional Chinese philosophy of Taoism speaks of a balance between the two life principles, yin and yang, both of which are needed for living beings to continue their existence. But yin and yang are seldom equally strong, and, according to Taoism, the constant interplay between the two is the ground of all life and development. The biological counterpart to that ancient philosophical view is the dynamic play between the systems of fight or flight and calm and connection. The former one is well-known, heavily researched, and overemphasized in our culture. Now it is time for the other life-preserving principle to be clearly identified and acknowledged.

Repairing and Restoring Balance

Newborn rats whose mothers did not get enough to eat during pregnancy have been shown to carry high levels of stress hormones. They have a normal birth weight, but they don't grow as they should later in life. However, administration of oxytocin injections to these young rats early in life helps them achieve normal levels of stress hormones and normal growth patterns.

A clear overload on the stress side of the see-saw can be balanced by activating the calm and connection effects. It is as if nature were telling us again and again that it is not a matter of "either/or." Living beings thrive best with a balance of "both/and." When we understand that, we are in better shape physically and psychologically.

This is hardly news. There are many traditional techniques of fostering calm and connection that have been worked out on the basis of experience, without the slightest knowledge of oxytocin or any other substances involved. But now we are beginning to discover, measure, and explain what is happening physiologically in such traditional practices as, for example, massage and other touch therapies, popular components of many wellness regimens. But before we study oxytocin's relation to touch more closely, we will first visit the place where oxytocin was discovered: the act of nursing.

8

Nursing: Oxytocin's Starring Role

Oxytocin was originally called the birthing and nursing hormone because it was first identified in this context. Over time, however, my colleagues and I have found that oxytocin has many more roles to play, and both females and males are influenced by it in a variety of situations. Nursing, however, is still a paradigm for the workings of oxytocin; it is also well researched, since it allows the effects of oxytocin to be studied without administering the substance from outside the body.

When a woman nurses a baby or a female animal suckles offspring, a great chain of events ensues. The breast or milk-producing organ is stimulated by the sucking of the infant. Nerve impulses travel from the breast to the supraoptic and the paraventricular cell groups in the hypothalamus, causing oxytocin to be released into the bloodstream. This blood-borne oxytocin reaches the so-called myoepithelial cells, organized muscle cells that lie next to the milk-producing cells in the breasts. These cells then contract and squeeze out the milk.

All this is a reflex action. When the reflex is triggered enough times by the nursing baby, it produces a learned, or conditioned, reflex. Then when the woman sees her baby, hears the infant cry, or even just thinks about him or her, she may experience a tightening in her breast from the pressure of the milk, which may even begin to flow.

This conditioned reflex happens not only in humans but in other animals. When a cow is milked by the same person day after day, the mere sight of that person or the sound of the clinking milk pail is often enough to make the cow's milk come.

During nursing, oxytocin also produces other effects. These have been confirmed by experiments that introduce a so-called oxytocin antagonist, a substance that counteracts the working of oxytocin by blocking its receptors so that the hormone has nowhere to attach. Without the vital oxytocin receptors, injections of oxytocin have no effect, and we can then see which of oxytocin's effects fail to show up.

As we saw earlier, the skin temperature on the side of a rat's body nearest her young rises when she is suckling them. In the same way, women experience a warming of the front torso when nursing; this is because oxytocin dilates the blood vessels in the skin on that part of the body. To survive, infants need not only nourishment but also warmth, care, and protection. This warming effect supplies one of these needs, and, as we will see, oxytocin also plays a role in the mother's urges to provide the other two.

Oxytocin and Milk

Because nature provides mother's milk as an infant's only food, there must be enough of it, and it must be nourishing. Oxytocin stimulates prolactin, a hormone from the frontal lobe of the hypothalamus that increases milk production. In addition, insulin, a hormone that primarily helps in the absorption of nutrients in the body's storage depots, has another function in the stimulation of milk production. Oxytocin plays an important role in increasing insulin production and changing its function during nursing. Oxytocin also influences the hormone glucagon, which stimulates the release of nutrients from the body's storage areas. In this way, the breasts are provided with enough resources to produce an abundant supply of milk.

It is not possible to give away nourishment if there is not enough surplus in one's own stores; therefore, frequent nursing must be combined with the conservation of nutrients, either in advance or at the time of the giving. Oxytocin helps the body store nutrients by, for example, increasing the appetite and promoting digestion and the effectiveness of the body's storage systems. This balance of nursing and conservation varies in individual women and explains why some nursing women lose weight and others gain pounds.

A gene has been discovered in certain mice that correlates with more oxytocin-producing cells in the hypothalamus. The mice with this gene produce more milk for their young and usually lose weight while nursing. Interestingly, this gene is inherited from the mother's father's side, meaning that "Grandpa" is making sure his daughter's babies consume enough milk. We do not yet know how this type of gene functions in humans.

Oxytocin and the Newborn Baby

Newborn babies nowadays are often placed skin-to-skin on the mother's chest immediately after delivery. If left to do as they please, they will crawl up to the mother's breast by themselves within one to two hours after birth and start to suckle or breastfeed. As they root around for the nipple, they massage the mother's breast with their hands. During this time, repeated pulses of oxytocin are released into the mother's system. It seems that the baby creates these pulses, since the stimulation of the breast by the baby's hands and the sucking activity are strongly (statistically significantly) correlated to the number of oxytocin pulses. These not only stimulate the ejection of milk but also dilate the blood vessels in the mother's chest. In this way, as we have seen, the mother provides warmth to the infant. It is also possible that pheromones are released at this time, influencing mother and baby.

This close, skin-to-skin contact also affects the babies. They become calmer and do not cry as long as they are allowed to stay on their mothers' chests. They show that they are relaxed through an increased blood flow in their hands and feet. (Blood vessels dilate in relaxation.) This nuanced interplay between mother and infant is also evident in the increased warmth in the baby's feet as well as in the mother's body temperature. The warmer the mother, the warmer the baby's feet.

The release of oxytocin has not been studied in newborns, but since the level of the stress hormone cortisol decreases, the level of oxytocin in the brain probably increases. Breastfeeding also enhances these effects. Other senses (hearing, smell, and sight, especially eye contact, which can be thought of as a kind of indirect touch) play an important role in this intricate choreography between mother and infant immediately after birth.

The Peace of Nursing

To an outside observer, the most noticeable effect of nursing is the mother's state of calmness and relaxation. This calmness can even be measured, both in humans and in laboratory rats. With nursing, blood pressure decreases, and the level of the stress hormone cortisol in the blood drops. This means that the activity of the sympathetic nervous system and the adrenal glands has diminished. The nursing female rat also responds to stressful stimuli with relatively less production of stress hormones. The more often a rat mother receives a dose of oxytocin, the longer these calming effects last.

Measurements of brain activity in nursing animals show that many sleep while they nurse their young; this is also often true of human mothers, especially when they nurse at night. The condition of deep mental calm is thus also associated with the period of nursing.

These behavioral and physiological changes are not short-lived, but persist throughout the entire period of breast-feeding or suckling. Although some women react differently, most nursing mothers are more composed and at peace with their surroundings than under other circumstances. Nursing rat females are less sensitive to disturbances than before.

During the period of nursing, many women experience a desire for a more peaceful life. Chores that were once important and had to be done end up farther down the list. Nursing mothers enjoy quiet and seclusion within the family; most do not consider nursing and child care boring and time consuming because they have less need for variety than usual. During my research, the nursing mothers who exhibited the greatest behavioral changes also had the highest levels of oxytocin in their blood. The number of oxytocin pulses in a single breast-feeding period is related not only to the amount of milk but also to the mother's level of calm.

As I discussed earlier, oxytocin circulates through two separate pathways, the bloodstream and the nervous system. Only when there are very high doses does the oxytocin in one system "spill over" into the other. For this reason, I believe that, in addition to the elevated level of the substance in the blood during the nursing period, the oxytocin level in the nervous system is increased. Since oxytocin in the brain fosters calm and relaxation, my colleagues and I have concluded that these changed behaviors are due to this increase of oxytocin released in the brain; we have also been able to show a connection between high oxytocin levels in the blood over time and the experience of calm, desire for seclusion, and less demand for variety in the environment.

Oxytocin and Cesarean Deliveries

Women whose babies have been delivered by cesarean section have on the average fewer oxytocin pulses in connection with breast-feeding two to three days after birth when compared with women who have delivered vaginally. The mothers after surgery are also generally less calm than mothers who delivered vaginally, and also less interactive with those around them. We do not know whether these differences are due to a reduced release of oxytocin during birth, delayed skin-to-skin contact after birth, or pain and stress caused by the surgery. Anesthesia and analgesics such as epidural blocks may also play a role. Whether given for cesarean section or for pain relief, they may affect the levels of oxytocin released during and after birth.

It is well known that mothers who have had cesarean sections tend to have more trouble with breast-feeding. Apparently, the development of the breast-feeding pattern and associated behavioral changes are delayed in these women, and statistical calculations indicate that the reduction in oxytocin plays an important role. It will be important to find out whether there are also long-term variations in the nature of the mother/infant relationship and whether any

negative effects on this bonding mechanism can be amelio-
rated.

Sucking and Emotional Bonding

As we saw, the effects of oxytocin in nursing extend to the
baby as well as the mother. The first interaction after birth
between infant and mother in the mammalian world is usually the baby's sucking, which provides the newborn both
food and contact. The sucking is also connected with social
memory. Newborn lambs that suckle immediately after
birth recognize their mothers more easily the following day
than lambs that are kept from immediate suckling. It
appears that the gastrointestinal hormone cholecystokinin
(CCK, which stimulates the contraction of the gall bladder)
is involved here; the positive effect from early suckling disappears if the lamb is treated with a CCK antagonist that
blocks its functioning. Since CCK leads to oxytocin release
in the brain, oxytocin is likely involved as well.

Calves that suckle have more oxytocin than those that
drink milk from a pail. It is thus not only food in the stomach that leads to the release of oxytocin with the help of
CCK; the act of sucking also triggers this causal chain of
events. It is not known to what extent human babies bond
with their mothers when first nursed, but current birthing
practice assumes a connection between early nursing and
attachment to the mother.

The effects of sucking itself can be seen in premature
babies. Those who are so weak that they must be fed through

a stomach tube become calmer and gain weight more rapidly if they also suck as much as possible on a small nipple.

Most parents know that small children are calmed by sucking on a pacifier or their own thumbs, even if the sucking does not provide a reward in the form of food. Nursing mothers likewise know that their babies are often calmed by sucking on the breast even if they are not especially hungry. The bonding to the breast, pacifier, or thumb gradually strengthens. Training children to eat other foods is not too difficult; with time they become hungrier and need more solid fare. But it is often much harder to wean the child away from a pacifier or thumb. Oxytocin and the consequent bonding are probably triggered by sucking because that action stimulates the inside of the mouth in much the same way that touch stimulates the outside skin.

Being with Others

Under the influence of the oxytocin system, not only do women in a maternal role become more peaceful but they also have an increased facility for and interest in certain sorts of interaction. Just as rat mothers build a nest, protect their young from danger, and keep them clean, so human mothers care for their children in comparable ways. They develop not only deep bonds to their children but also closeness to certain others, especially within their inner circle. The women interviewed for my research enjoyed the company of close friends and family and relaxing communication.

This increased closeness does not correlate with the oxy-tocin level in general, but with short, repeated increases of its concentration in the blood. Thus, the more the oxytocin level spikes, the stronger is the facility for interaction. Women who have more of this spiking also produce more milk and nurse for a longer time.

It is important to note here that there are, of course, many differences among women. The nursing experience is influenced by such factors as personality, heredity, difficulty of the delivery, and other life circumstances. For example, some women may experience depression and anxiety during nursing because of an innate vulnerability, unfortunate childhood experiences, or lack of a supportive partner.

In summary, oxytocin generally influences the nursing woman's psyche in two ways: She becomes calmer, enjoying seclusion, but she is also more open to close, interpersonal contact. Both these adaptations are of considerable value during nursing and must surely be important from an evo-lutionary point of view.

In the next chapter I will look more closely at the role played by the skin as a mediating link between the outside world's stimuli and oxytocin's many effects, and explain why humans and animals clearly benefit from touch.

OXYTOCIN'S ROLE IN NURSING

1. Controls the expulsion of milk
2. Stimulates milk production
3. Redistributes heat in the mother's body to warm the nursing young
4. Helps the body release stored nutrients
5. Increases the mother's ability to extract nutrition in the digestive process
6. Reduces blood pressure and stress hormones in the mother
7. Creates calm in most nursing women in proportion to the oxytocin levels in their blood
8. Makes the mother more interested in close relationships. The more spikes in oxytocin content in her blood, the more open to attachment and bonding she becomes
9. Induces social memory and calmness in the infant

PART FOUR

Connections

9

Oxytocin and Touch

The skin of both humans and animals is constantly passing information from the outside world to the nervous system. This largest sensory organ in humans and most mammals registers warmth, cold, touch, and pain. Each of these sensations is picked up by receptors connected to the sensory nervous system, which conveys the impulses to the central nervous system (described in Chapter 4).

Thanks to this amazing sense organ, we can quickly interpret messages from the world around us, whether threatening or pleasant. Without effort, we can distinguish between a cruel poke or a friendly stroke. We sweat or get goose bumps, depending on signals sent through our central nervous system.

The Dual Effects of Touch

The skin has different types of receptors, some to register pain, others warmth, and still others light touching. When the pain receptors are stimulated by a heavy-handed touch or blow, or by excessive heat, a nerve message about this noxious stimulus is sent to the brain. This message, in turn, sets in motion other reactions: We instinctively try to ward off the pain or escape from it by such actions as jerking our hands away or drawing back. The pain is followed in that case by the body's reflexive flight reaction.

More recent research shows that touch can also activate an entirely different set of responses from this heavily studied and extremely familiar flight response. Pleasant touch and warmth activate the calm and connection system, bringing on a feeling of well-being. These effects are not felt as immediately as those of the fight or flight system, but they often last longer.

When nerves responsive to pain and touch were stimulated in anesthetized rats, the activity in the sympathetic nervous system increased, followed by a rise in blood pressure and heart rate. Levels of the stress hormones noradrenaline, adrenaline, and cortisol also increased. In contrast, when the nerves that convey information about pleasant touch and warmth were stimulated, the result was lower blood pressure and decreased levels of stress hormones. At the same time, levels of several of the digestive hormones controlled by the parasympathetic nervous system, such as insulin, rose, as did the level of oxytocin.

When the animals were deeply sedated, they were unaware of either pleasant or unpleasant sensations, so any affects on their movement patterns could not be ascertained. When a painful stimulus was administered to a wakeful rat, it struck out or tried to run away, or even froze in place. When the wakeful rats were stroked on the stomach with a specific amount of pressure at a certain frequency, they became less sensitive to pain and less fearful. A rate of forty strokes per minute for just under five minutes proved to have the most pronounced effect. The rats also became calmer and less active, as well as more curious and interested in each other. Their blood pressure decreased and remained lower for several hours.

In the above experiments, the stimulation of different sensory nerves was able to evoke either the fight or flight reaction or the calm and connection response. This means that both these systems can be set in motion through sensory receptors in the skin in most areas of the body, and these different kinds of stimuli can produce different effects on both physiology and behavior. As we will see, these effects have useful implications for both medical and psychological therapies.

Oxytocin as the Key

We saw in the previous chapter that nursing women and suckling mammals become calmer and less stressed, and the research on skin receptors shows that this is not the only kind of physical stimulation that produces the same effect. Touch can, under certain conditions, also elicit similar reactions in both females and males. Since oxytocin injections also produce this effect, we can speculate that it must be the release of oxytocin through touch that activates the calm and connection reaction, including the changes in behavior as well as lowered blood pressure and pulse rate.

A dramatic effect of touch in animals has been demonstrated by a German dairy farmer who designed a body brush for his cows. Similar to a car wash, but dry, the machine gives the cows a delightful stroking sensation. They become relaxed, appear to be in better condition, and produce up to 26 percent more milk. This link between touch and oxytocin was confirmed by other experiments: Oxytocin levels regularly rose in the blood and brain in connection with different types of repetitive and soothing stimulation that was delivered by activating certain nerves in sedated rats or by stroking the stomachs of wakeful animals. The effect became more powerful if the stimulation was repeated multiple times.

These calming effects appear after a certain delay and can persist long after the last application. Thus, different kinds of touch influence the oxytocin system in the same way as actual injections of oxytocin do. As further confirmation of the link between touch and oxytocin, when rats in the above experiments were given an oxytocin antagonist, an elevated pain threshold effect failed to appear.

One interesting finding in these same experiments is that it appears to be easier to induce the calm and connection effect by stroking the front side of the animal rather than the dorsal side. For example, it was much easier to lower blood pressure with frontal stroking. It is quite likely that the back is more connected with defensive mechanisms, since from that side of the body it is harder to see what is going on and evaluate the danger of a situation. As is true in connection with nursing, special nerves go from the skin on the frontal side into the central nervous system via the vagus nerve. These nerves do not pass through the spinal cord, but go directly to the brain. Perhaps the presence of these direct nerve connections explains why stroking on the stomach in the above experiment was more effective than stroking on the back. However, when I discuss massage, I will explain how, at least in human beings, a back rub can send powerfully calming messages to the nervous system.

Touch and Growth

Regular, pleasant touch not only produces calm but also improves growth. Baby rats separated from their mothers grow less satisfactorily than those that continue to receive their mothers' care, including touching. When the isolated young rats are stroked with a soft brush, however, they show improvement in their growth. Even adult rats whose growth is retarded through reaction to stress can regain lost ground with similar treatment.

Touch is beneficial for human growth and health. For decades, studies of institutionalized children have shown that food alone is not sufficient to produce healthy growth. Touch also is needed; without it, the children's digestive processes are disrupted and they become too thin even if they are getting enough food. This condition, called "failure to thrive," can be life-threatening.

One explanation for this link between touch and growth has been an increased release of growth hormone from the pituitary gland. Oxytocin also appears to be involved, since, as mentioned earlier, it influences the secretion of growth hormone and the body's ability to store nutrients.

THE EFFECTS OF PLEASANT TOUCH

Pleasant touch, at a rate of about forty times per minute, has produced the following effects in experiments with rats:

- lower blood pressure;
- higher pain threshold (increased tolerance for pain);
- lower level of stress hormones;
- lower tail temperature;
- increased growth in both young and adult animals;
- increased social interaction; and
- improved learning.

These reactions, which coincide with the effects of oxytocin injections, become sustained with repetition of the touch stimulus or injections.

10

Oxytocin and Other Senses

It is easy to understand, even for someone unfamiliar with medical science, that touch can calm us and that certain substances can be released in the body through activation of touch receptors in the skin. But it is a little more difficult to accept that a similar chain of events can occur with the other senses.

Input from our organs of smell, taste, hearing, and sight most likely influences our physiological reactions to a much greater extent than commonly thought. When we think about it, this is not so far-fetched. We talk about being able to smell danger, or we experience a sound that makes us uneasy, or we see an "alarming" sight. What if we can also be calmed and relaxed physiologically by input from our senses? A related question is whether such effects also work by causing the release of oxytocin. Several interesting research results imply that they do.

We saw that administering oxytocin to an individual rat produces certain effects, such as an elevated pain threshold. But surprisingly, to a lesser degree, *animals that live in the same cage but have not directly received oxytocin also show the same changes.* The other animals in the cage become calmer and have lower levels of stress hormones, just as the rats who actually received oxytocin did. Since giving these other animals an oxytocin antagonist eliminates this effect, it appears that their oxytocin system is definitely involved.

Because this effect also disappears if the olfactory ability of the untreated rats is temporarily blocked, the transmission probably occurs through smell, which in turn activates the oxytocin system. Thus oxytocin's effects can be spread not only between two individuals through touch but among many individuals through odor. Other animal experiments show that calm and connection can be produced by way of other senses as well.

It is extremely likely that the transfer of this so-called "smell effect" happens with humans. We know that we almost all like certain aromas—a tiny infant, fresh-baked pie, lilies of the valley. We also know that most of us dislike other smells, such as rotten meat or days-old sweat. But there are other odors of which we are not conscious that influence us as well. These effects are not necessarily produced via the regular organ of smell. As mentioned in Chapter 4, we have another means of smell, the vomeronasal organ, which is probably much older from an evolutionary perspective.

This special sense organ takes in pheromones, substances that are transmitted through the air from one individual to another. The nerves associated with their effects do not go directly to the cerebral cortex and the olfactory bulb; instead, they lead to older parts of the brain, from which body functions and emotions are partially controlled. (See Figure 4.3.)

A person can thus be powerfully influenced by pheromones without being conscious of it. When we have trouble establishing a good relationship with someone no matter what we do, or when we are afraid of someone without really knowing why, it is possible that these odors are involved in our reactions. When two people are sexually attracted to each other, pheromones and the vomero-nasal organ probably play a significant role in the power of the emotions they feel. I believe that oxytocin is probably also involved with these subtle olfactory signals in some way as yet undiscovered.

Researchers have not yet measured the release of oxytocin in connection with restful sounds or with the sight of something lovely, but common experience shows that pleasant music and beautiful scenery can be enormously calming. There are even techniques for using music not only to promote relaxation but to improve learning. Animals produce different kinds of calls that have certain physiological effects, such as between a mother and her young, between members of a mating pair, or among all the animals in a group. We humans are also influenced by certain wordless sounds, such as shouts or groans, as well as facial expressions. A shrill, loud voice or an angry grimace is unsettling, but a friendly tone or look promotes calm and pleasant communication.

Thus, all our senses are constantly involved in interpreting our immediate environment. If we sense it to be threatening and dangerous, our fight or flight reaction is evoked; but if we interpret it to be pleasant and peaceful, we have a response of calm and connection.

11

Oxytocin and Sexuality

"Love is all you need," sang the Beatles in the sexually liberated 1960s. They weren't so very wrong. The act of love probably has a whole series of healthful effects, including its ability to make us feel calm and relaxed afterward. This calm, as well as the touch and connection involved in lovemaking, increases our output of oxytocin, which in turn facilitates healing, aids digestion, and produces other anti-stress effects.

Oxytocin very likely plays a key role in human sexual behavior, in part because of the intensive touching and oral stimulation of kissing involved, but also because orgasm itself releases a flood of oxytocin into the bloodstream. This is known both as a result of animal experiments and because measurements have been taken in human research subjects after intercourse.

Because we've observed that injections of oxytocin in laboratory rats facilitate mating in several ways, we can conclude that natural oxytocin influences mating behavior as well. Oxytocin stimulates the release of eggs from the ovaries, assists in their transport through the tubes to the uterus, and aids in the production and transport of sperm. Since growth is oxytocin's fundamental principle, what could be more logical than the substance's connection with eggs, sperm, and fertility?

The Peak of Orgasm

Some studies of human sexual relations have shown that oxytocin levels rise powerfully in the blood of both males and females and reach maximum concentration with the release of orgasm. Oxytocin may also stimulate the muscle activity related to orgasm in both women and men.

After sexual intercourse, we often feel calm, relaxed, and even drowsy. Sometimes, we take the greatest pleasure from our partner's closeness then, when all tension has vanished and nothing feels more important than to be near our beloved. The biochemical explanation for this is probably oxytocin's direct and indirect effects on the body and certain areas of the brain.

Experiments show that large amounts of oxytocin make animals fall asleep; lower doses make them unafraid, calm, and interested in contact with other animals. When oxytocin levels return to balance shortly after orgasm, lovers become wide awake again and they look at one another. Now he or she may have faults or failings, but—how wonderful this person is to make love with and be close to! With oxytocin pulsating through the bloodstream, it seems that this love will last forever. Often at this point, partners speak of how much they mean to each other.

These effects of oxytocin are influenced, however, by the conditions under which the sexual encounter takes place. The more the encounter contains an element of tension and danger, the more it is influenced by oxytocin's sister substance, vasopressin, and so a stress reaction is produced. An extreme example, which deserves mention here, is sexual activity involving some sort of pain or violence. This type of sex might calm the individual momentarily, immediately after orgasm, but it is probably experienced by the body at least in part as an attack. This reaction then activates the aggression and defense mechanisms in the form of higher blood pressure, tightened muscles, and even reduced emotional responses and desensitization to touch.

Most of us know how our bond with another person is strengthened when we make love. Although mothers of all generations have warned their daughters against having sex outside traditionally acceptable circumstances for fear of an unwanted pregnancy, perhaps, in light of our knowledge of oxytocin's effects, they should add another warning. Pregnancy can be protected against, but there are no pills (at least not in today's pharmacies) to prevent the bonding that accompanies an intimate relationship, thanks to oxytocin. There is always a risk that emotional bonds will become powerful before the partners know enough to be sure that they are right for each other.

Sex and Health

In the short term, each sexual encounter includes an element of stress. But in the long run, a solid sexual relationship promotes feelings of increased security and decreased anxiety in the mating partners. The repeated bursts of oxytocin evoke the long-term effects usually associated with the calm and connection system. Through these effects, sexual activity has a positive impact on health by promoting nutritional balance, healing, and the restoration of biological resources. Statistical studies also indicate that secure, long-term sexual relationships contribute to a longer life span for males. (Women appear to have found other ways to provide themselves with oxytocin.) On the other hand, having sex with a stranger (in prostitution, for example) contains a certain amount of danger, something that the body registers by initiating a form of the fight or flight reaction instead of the calm and connection system. Then the healthful oxytocin-related effects of sexual activity are counteracted, or at least neutralized. It is therefore possible that monogamy and the cultural taboo against infidelity have, at least in part, a biologically adaptive basis.

Oxytocin and Relationships

We feel good when we're near people we like. Whether we are babies or grown-ups, physical closeness and touch provide us with a feeling of security, help us relax and calm down. It is not only the small child seeking a hug from mama or papa who needs physical contact; adults also need it in their relationships if they are to feel cared for.

People have known this since the time of Adam and Eve. But now, for the first time, science is beginning to find out what actually happens physiologically to make close relationships good for our well-being. It's not only the emotional experiences of love and security that make us feel good. Closeness and physical contact also activate physiological processes in our bodies in a way that is healthy for us.

Bonding Relationships

In experiments with rats, injections of oxytocin promote various kinds of physical closeness: maternal behavior, sexual activity, and varying degrees of social interaction. The animals sit closer to each other, sniff each other, and groom each others' fur more often. These activities set in motion a positive cycle of effects and lead to increased secretion of the animals' own oxytocin, which, in its turn, promotes more interaction. With some species of animals, this dynamic results in what can be called bonding between individuals.

Although many animals recognize each other and develop a familiarity, only a few species of mammals are monogamous in the sense that the male and the female bond with each other for life. In contrast, it is important for all nursing animals to establish a strong two-way bond between the mother and her young; the species' survival depends on their ability to recognize and stay connected with each other.

With sheep, the hour after birth is extremely important for bonding between the ewe and the lamb. If they are separated during this sensitive time, they have more difficulty bonding with each other, and the ewe will often reject the lamb. After an injection of oxytocin, the ewe might accept not only her own lamb, even at a later time, but also the off-spring of another ewe, and will develop a maternal relationship with them. We can thus conclude that oxytocin plays an important role in the bonding between a mother and her offspring, especially directly after birth.

This premise is supported by the results of another experiment: When an oxytocin antagonist was given to a ewe during the birthing process, her maternal behavior and the bonding process did not develop. The same was true if she received a spinal anesthetic during delivery, since this procedure blocks the release of oxytocin. Oxytocin is thus fundamental to the first bonding in these mammals' lives. Only if the ewe and lamb can recognize each other and the mother lets the infant suckle will the next generation survive.

As I mentioned earlier, not only will female rats become motherly with the help of oxytocin but they will even take care of young rats they have never seen before. We have also seen that oxytocin is released in human females as a consequence of the newborn's first handling of the breast and first attempt to suck. This increased oxytocin is important not only for milk production but also for the development of a loving bond between mother and child.

Oxytocin is also an important factor in other types of bonding besides that of mother and child. If bonding is typical for a species, then high oxytocin levels increase the tendency of adult males and females to bond. A certain type of vole is known for creating stable pairings. When a female of this species is placed with a certain male while she is receiving an oxytocin injection, she later tends to prefer him even if she can have her choice of several other males. He becomes her "one in a million." Oxytocin thus facilitates bonding in mating as well as in parental situations.

Touch and Bonding

Just as oxytocin reduces aggression and fear in rats, I believe that humans are more open to interpersonal contact when oxytocin is involved. Touch and physical contact initiate a reinforcing cycle and produce increased secretion of oxytocin; this makes us more curious and interested in establishing contact, and, this in its turn, releases still more oxytocin, and so on. As shown in our animal experiments, a cycle is created that leads to the establishment of an emotional bond between individuals.

Caring for small children offers many possibilities for stroking and cuddling, and because of this they usually experience a great deal of parental touching. This sort of physical contact increases feelings of security and closeness between parent and child. Even though touch is not experienced so intensively later in a child's life, early handling in a warm and loving manner helps us approach later relationships with a continued sense of connection and trust. These later relationships marked by bonding and closeness are good not only for our emotional well-being but also for our physical health.

Touch and Childbirth

Most of us prefer to have physical contact only with people we know well. A woman in childbirth labor, however, is often glad to have a stranger rub her back or touch her in some other way. Studies of labor companions, known as "doulas," have shown that such support speeds delivery and reduces the experience of pain for women in labor.

A doula touches, holds, and supports a woman during labor, physically as well as mentally. Studies done by Marshall Klaus and John Kennell, doctors whose research has influenced childbirth practice in U.S. hospitals, have shown that with this care, the need for pain relief is significantly reduced. Also, the mothers see the experience of labor in a more positive light. Recently, several studies have been published showing that the presence of a doula has long-term effects. Six weeks after birth, the mothers who had support from a doula have a better relationship with their infants, and also with their partners, than mothers who did not have this support. There are also fewer incidences of depression among these mothers. It is possible that an enhanced release of oxytocin, brought about by the combination of touch and close emotional support provided by a doula, is behind the beneficial effect on the progress of labor and the mother/baby bonding.

The results of these studies can be interpreted in a more general way. They demonstrate that openness to new and positive experience is substantial when levels of oxytocin are high, as they are during labor. Under such circumstances, it seems that loving and nurturing care can influence the individual in a very deep and sustained way. Perhaps touch, warmth, and support induce changes in the brain similar to those that are induced by repeated administration of oxytocin in animal experiments. In any event, these studies show that important positive psychophysiological changes can be induced without drugs.

As we will see in Part 5, there are many nonmedical ways of bringing about these effects. It is possible to elevate oxytocin levels in both men and women by giving a combination of stimuli such as warmth, touch, massage, rhythmic motion, and supportive and friendly psychological feedback. The lessons we have learned about the importance of caring support in childbirth may be useful in other types of therapeutic situations.

Touch in a Variety of Relationships

When we are sick or in need, we are calmed by the touch of a doctor or nurse, even one we do not know. To have our hand held or to be stroked or even hugged by a caregiver, even if we have never seen the person before, often feels entirely appropriate when we are not feeling well or are in some other way vulnerable. Studies have also shown that a nurse's touch lowers the pulse rate in an acutely ill patient, even though it raises the pulse rate in a healthy person.

Generally, however, touch is associated with close relationships between people who already know each other. You show your feelings with touch and convey information without words, often without thinking about it. You pat your friend encouragingly on the shoulder to show that you believe in him even if no one else does. When you are with your lover, you tenderly caress his naked back without thinking about it. You stroke the silken cheek of your small child and hold her by the hand when the two of you are walking together.

Types of touch differ in close relationships, whether of parent and child, siblings, sexual partners, or friends. Since we now know that touch and physical contact cause the release of oxytocin, we can feel confident that a relationship between two people that includes mutual pleasant touch not only creates an emotional bonding but also transmits the positive health and antistress effects of oxytocin.

It is as important for survival to be able to be close to someone as it is to be able to defend yourself against someone. Just as we have many culturally acceptable ways of expressing aggression and boundary setting, we also have various standard ways to promote the release of oxytocin through bodily contact. Most families engage in physical contact, which occurs between parents and children and between siblings, even up to adulthood. Strong bonds between friends are often expressed through hugs and kisses. Though this may sometimes be ritualized as "blowing kisses," the message remains that bodily contact is an integral part of a safe and friendly relationship.

Even workplace colleagues or team members in sports feel a kinship and group identity that can be expressed through touch and promoted by physical contact. Think of a cheering team rushing a goal scorer and nearly fighting over who gets to hug him or her! Sometimes, touch outside the private sphere is a significant means of creating connection and trust. One interesting experiment studied the check-out process in a library and found that borrowers who had been lightly touched by the librarian returned their books at a much higher rate than those who had not been touched. This light contact created an emotional connection that encouraged the borrower to return the book. A person who is touched is more likely to honor a promise.

We feel a connection as well with someone who gives us a facial treatment, a massage, or a pedicure. These modes of touching often promote a sense of closeness; we may even be inclined to unload our troubles onto a person toward whom we have developed such feelings.

Of course, there are wide cultural differences in acceptable forms of touch. Studies have shown that the French touch each other more than Americans would in the same situations. It is possible that this cultural difference may be correlated with certain differences in health and illness.

Psychological Contact

Relationships and encounters can give us the experience of touch on a psychological level, even without bodily contact. A meeting or a communication with another person can be experienced either as warm and supportive or as chilly and demanding. Someone who listens attentively to us gives us a feeling of confidence and connection, just as a friendly touch does. Our perception of a relationship, the way we experience it, determines to what extent our fight or flight reaction or our calm and connection response is triggered. The situation will then bear the stamp of either vasopressin or oxytocin.

A relationship is difficult and can be destructive if its signals are ambiguous or unclear, especially if the situation should offer security but does not, as in domestic violence or child abuse. A less common turn of events is the relationship that changes from threatening and antagonistic to comforting and friendly.

Absence of Touch

We customarily regard the stress of separation as unhealthy. Such stress can lead to illness, in part because of its connection to the hyperactivity of the sympathetic nervous system. A separation from someone we are close to, whether it is voluntary or involuntary, has powerful stress effects. There are demonstrable connections between separation and illness, including statistics that show that a person who has recently lost a spouse runs a greater risk of becoming sick. The related effects, such as elevated blood pressure, a rapid heartbeat, disturbances of heart rhythm, and an increased tendency for the blood to coagulate, can produce cardiovascular disease and stroke (bleeding or blood clotting in the brain).

An important part of the stress of losing a personal connection through death or separation may be the sudden loss of touch and consequently of many of the effects that closeness and warmth generate. When these healthful stimuli disappear, the risk of illness grows.

Healthful Effects of Good Relationships

The oxytocin that good relationships produce is our personal healing nectar. Several studies have shown that positive personal relationships are conducive to a longer life. People who reported that they had good relationships in general were also healthier, the males especially showing a lower incidence of cardiovascular disease. The reverse is also true; if a woman experiences her marriage as negative and stressful, cardiovascular disease worsens.

These relationships do not need to be intimate to be good for us. Even affiliations with groups and communal activities can have a positive effect on health. Sports and competitions can have these effects, but they also can be filled with stress and disappointment. We can deal with this kind of challenge occasionally, but when it becomes a chronic condition, it can have negative consequences.

Friendly relationships with animals also promote health. Dog owners, for example, have lower than average blood pressure, perhaps because of the exercise they get from walking their dogs as well as the touch and physical contact that the relationships with their pets include. Even some people with psychological illnesses such as schizophrenia have shown an improved ability to interact socially when they live with a dog or a cat. Perhaps children's chores with animals—currying horses or caring for rabbits, for example—can have a positive effect on their health and social skills, although these findings are still speculative.

Relationship to a Place

Can the calm and connection reaction be triggered by other circumstances that do not necessarily include contact with

OXYTOCIN AND RELATIONSHIPS

1. Touch releases oxytocin in animals and probably also in humans.
2. The release of oxytocin creates emotional bonds between people, such as mother and child.
3. Good relationships are important for health, especially with respect to diseases of the cardiovascular system. Breast cancer survival has also been shown to be longer in women with close relationships.
4. Good relationships probably stimulate the calm and connection system, not only through touch but also through feelings of support, warmth, and love.
5. Even certain places that we "have a relation to" can have a calming influence, probably by activating the oxytocin system.

living beings? Young animals appear generally calm and secure in their nests or cages even if the mother is not there, because the information they get through their senses of sight, hearing, smell, and touch is "right" and feels like home. Perhaps their oxytocin is released because these messages *remind them of mama,* just as the nursing mother's oxytocin is released when she hears her child's cry or as the cow's milk begins to run when the farmer rattles the milking machine. This kind of stimulus can cause the release of oxytocin through a conditioned reflex.

In the same way, home, especially a childhood home or hometown, can have a calming effect on people in a way that may be linked to the physiological system described in this book. This type of home is not associated with an absent mother, but with the positive experiences of calm and security that we learn to connect with it. Many people return to live in their hometowns when they are growing older, perhaps because they feel more secure there than anywhere else. It is also well known that people who, because of old age, are forced to leave their homes of many years often decline both physically and mentally as a result of this separation. A patient, especially a very sick one, experiences home care as less stressful than receiving the same care in a hospital, because a familiar setting is calming.

PART FIVE

The Ways We Seek
Calm and Connection

13

Massage

Techniques of touch and massage have been used in many cultures for thousands of years as a way to achieve relaxation and calm. They have few unwanted effects, at least in healthy individuals. Until recently, people knew nothing about the biochemical profile of relaxation or the significance of touch in activating the calm and connection system, but they could see that those who were massaged emerged with rosy cheeks and a relaxed smile. Thus, much experience-based knowledge of massage has existed for a long time.

We now know that the gentle touching of animals leads to the release of oxytocin and the activation of the calm and connection system. Steers can be kept calm (as seen at country fairs in the United States) by stroking their chests in a gentle rhythmic motion with a long, blunt metal rod. The same likely also happens with humans. These physiological effects explain why experience-based techniques of touch have developed.

Many studies of massage's effects, however, are hard to interpret. Some have not used a control group of individuals who did not receive massage to compare with the ones who did. But even if we filter out research that in one way or another is not up to experimental standards, enough studies remain to demonstrate clearly that massage usually has obvious healthful effects on humans.

There are many types of massage. Some treatment techniques, such as tactile massage, involve touching only the skin. In other forms of massage, the muscles are thoroughly kneaded or just relaxed through the soft and light pressure of the therapist's hand. Obviously, these treatments activate different sensory nerves and thus to some extent lead to different outcomes; this has naturally added to the difficulty of measuring and interpreting the actual effects of massage. The relationship between the massage giver and the client can also vary.

At the Touch Research Institute (TRI) in Miami, founded by Tiffany Field, researchers examining the effects of touch, especially classic massage of the skin and muscles, have demonstrated that massage generally has an anxiety-reducing, calming, and relaxing effect on children and adults. For example, experiments in a juvenile psychiatric clinic showed that regular massage made the young patients calmer, less depressed and anxious, and more cooperative than the members of a control group were.

Levels of the stress hormone cortisol have been shown to fall in adults who receive massage, and these adults feel less anxious. Another experiment showed that it was easier to solve math problems quickly and correctly following a massage.

All these effects are similar to the effects of oxytocin injection that we saw in animal experiments: lower blood pressure, less cortisol, lower anxiety level, and more effective learning. As mentioned earlier, the effects of oxytocin are more powerful and long-lasting after repeated injections, and the same can be true after a series of massage treatments.

Massage and Skin Contact

Premature babies thrive better if they have extensive skin contact with their mothers, but such fragile little beings need touch more in the form of an embrace than a massage. The so-called kangaroo method of holding the baby against the mother's chest inside her clothes often works better than an incubator. Some premature babies grow stronger and develop more quickly if they receive very gentle massage, which must be carefully applied to avoid overburdening the nervous system. The massaged babies gain weight more quickly than other infants who receive the same amount of food. The cortisol levels in their blood also drop, an indication that they are less stressed.

Studies of massage in Swedish day care centers and schools indicate that incorporating massage into the daily routine produces a more peaceful group dynamic. One study of over one hundred young children showed that, with massage, the youngsters became calmer and more socially mature. After only three months, halfway through the study, parents and staff members noticed that the children's behavior was less aggressive. At the end of six months, there was no doubt at all that the children who received massage had changed for the better. They interacted better with their classmates and had fewer physical complaints at home. After nine months, a follow-up study showed that the effects were not only still evident but had become more pronounced with time.

Interestingly, the children who responded best to the regimen were the most disruptive boys, whose behavior during the study became less aggressive and more socially acceptable than that of comparable children who did not receive massage. Through the innate wisdom of the calm and connection system, the children who were already calm by nature were not affected as much by a little massage as were those who needed more calm and loving touch in their lives.

Because of the classic tradition of Swedish massage, this technique is more easily accepted by parents, teachers, and child care workers in Sweden than it would be in many other countries. In the United States, for example, it is barely permissible for a teacher to touch students, except to shake hands.

In this regard, it is important to note that the children are always asked whether they would like to have a massage.

In this way, they learn that they can control their own bodily integrity and set limits about what feels right to them. Children need to understand that they have a right to say yes or no to the touch of another person, whether a child or an adult.

Massage that is voluntary and closely structured can provide an important element in the relationship between children and school or day care personnel. It can compensate to an extent for the decline in physical contact inherent in our modern lifestyle, and it can counteract to some degree the increased stress that affects children and adults. If teachers and nursery school and child care workers could be taught to administer a basic form of massage and weave it into their lessons and activities, the children could become more relaxed and the group dynamic could function better.

Massage in Institutional Settings

In hospital settings, a special form of massage that is easy to apply has been tested on patients suffering from physical pain. This so-called tactile massage or stimulation is administered less deeply than other massage treatments and probably works primarily through the effect of touch on the skin. Little-publicized but convincing studies have shown that older patients who receive tactile massage sleep better, experience less pain, need less medication, and sometimes become less confused, more alert, and more sociable. Relationships with caregivers also improve. Because we know how rhythmic massage influences animals, it is not surprising to see these similar effects in humans.

Some studies show that oxytocin is released not only in the person receiving the massage, but in the person administering it as well. Massage therapists show typical effects of a high level of oxytocin, such as lower levels of stress hormones and lower blood pressure. Such people often enjoy a general well-being, perhaps related to the nature of their work.

Antistress

There is much about our modern lifestyle that limits the spontaneous release of natural oxytocin. We spend less time in close contact with others, either physically or psychologically, and we devote more time to work or other pursuits. The increased tempo of work and community activities means we rarely have the time or energy just to be close with each other, to walk hand in hand with a little one, or to devote a day to our love partner.

Without contact, we have less touch, and without touch, we have less oxytocin. Today, violence and aggression among young people are symptoms of a huge problem. Children are reported to be more disruptive and aggressive, and less able to concentrate, than they were even ten years ago. Our younger generation truly needs more calm and connection.

As we come to understand the importance of balancing stress with calm and relaxation, we can consciously choose

THE EFFECTS OF MASSAGE

1. Adults who receive massage have lower blood pressure, lower pulse rate, and lower levels of stress hormones, effects that promote health.
2. Children who receive massage become calmer, more socially mature, and less aggressive, and have fewer physical complaints.
3. Premature babies gain weight more rapidly if they receive gentle, embracing touch.

to pursue activities that release oxytocin without negative side effects. Taking a warm bath or a sauna, relaxing in the sun, getting a full body massage or even just a foot rub—these and many other such activities can help us wind down and enjoy oxytocin's pleasant effects in our bodies.

14

Eating: An Internal Massage

An old saying tells us that no problem is so big that a hearty meal won't solve it. It does often feel as though problems disappear while we are eating. At least, it is certainly true that what may be bothering us seems a little less problematic when we lean back, full and satisfied, after a good dinner. We become calmer and more content when we have eaten well because food and fullness provide another way to activate the body's calm and connection system.

The inside of the body is stimulated by eating, just as the outside is by touch. By eating, we actually activate the same calm and connection system. Because there are some interesting parallels between the digestive system and the skin, I sometimes think of eating as a sort of internal massage.

We can see how the skin and the digestive apparatus are related if we go far enough back in their cells' genealogical charts. During the first days of development after fertil-

ization of a human egg, the cells rapidly organize themselves into three groups of so-called germ layers; from
these, the entire fetus continues to develop. These three
germ layers are called the ectoderm, the mesoderm, and
the endoderm.

The gastrointestinal organs, the skin, and the nervous
system all develop from the same germ layer, the ectoderm.
It is not surprising, then, that there are functional similarities between the skin and the gastrointestinal system, for
example, in the way information from sensory nerves is registered and transmitted. We could even go so far as to say
that the digestive system, including the esophagus, stomach, and bowels, is like an inward continuation of the skin,
a sort of "outside-in," crunched-together exterior that has
become part of our unseen interior.

Not only is the gastrointestinal system important for
digestion but it is also one of the body's most significant
endocrine organs. It secretes hormones that regulate digestion, metabolism, and the storage of nutrients in the body's
cellular depots.

These hormones also have another function, namely, to
influence the brain. In the same way that the skin is richly
supplied with nerves, the gastrointestinal system has many
sympathetic and parasympathetic nerves. The nerve that
serves the greatest part of the gastrointestinal system is the
parasympathetic vagus nerve, which is 90 percent sensory
in function and carries impulses from the body's periphery
and interior to the central nervous system.

Between Gut and Brain

Picture yourself sitting at the table, ravenously hungry and salivating at the mere sight of the menu. You put the bites of food in your mouth, chew, and swallow. The food is entering your gastrointestinal system while you are most likely thinking of other things. By the time you start to feel that you are getting full, things have begun to happen inside your body.

Like the sensory nerve fibers in the skin that convey information through touch, the sensory fibers in the gastrointestinal system are of varying thickness and convey information of many different types. Such factors as the extent of stomach distension (that is, how much you have eaten), the pH level (degree of acidity), the amount of salt, and the presence of food of different chemical composition or calorie content can induce sensory activity in these nerves.

This activity conveys sensory information to the central nervous system about how things are going with the digestive process. We are never aware of most of this information, since almost all of it goes directly to the lower parts of the brain. Only in unusual circumstances, and then after a certain delay, do the signals go to the cerebral cortex, the part of the brain where we consciously register how we feel and where we think and plan. Gastrointestinal functioning is primarily autonomic, meaning that our intestines do their job without instructions from our conscious minds.

Among the messages the brain receives is information about how much food we have eaten, conveyed in part by secretion of the digestive hormone cholecystokinin (CCK). This hormone is released from the upper part of the small intestine when food, especially food with a high fat content, reaches that point. The CCK hormone activates the vagus nerve, which in turn stimulates the release of oxytocin. Thus the more fat a meal contains, the fuller and drowsier we feel afterward. When a meal consists of primarily carbohydrates and protein, the secretion of CCK is lower and the eater does not become so drowsy. Carbohydrates, and especially sugar, provide the quickest stimulation, at least temporarily.

The "inner touch" of the swallowed food on our internal organs thus leads to release of oxytocin in the brain, even though the reaction is first triggered by CCK in the gastrointestinal organs. As further evidence that CCK influences the release of oxytocin, a female rat treated with CCK and estrogen exhibits maternal and nurturing behavior, just as she would with oxytocin injections. Fullness therefore causes a release of oxytocin in the brain that leads to caring and friendly behavior.

Cows that are fed at the same time as they are milked become calmer and more sociable, and produce more milk. Activation of the vagus nerve by the act of eating leads to increased oxytocin secretion, resulting in these effects on the cow. Knowledge of this dynamic can be very useful in working with these animals.

Full and Content

In a certain way, we can say that the very early connection between food, emotional closeness, and bonding seen in babies lasts throughout life. When we have just eaten, our nagging hunger has gone. We feel untroubled and calm. It often feels good to lie down and rest a little, if we can. This feeling promotes very adaptive behavior, since when we rest, we more effectively digest the food and store its nutrients. The pleasant feeling of fullness is also good for our social relationships (if we do not become so full that we fall asleep, of course). When we are full, we have a more positive attitude toward our surroundings than when we are famished and feel upset and irritable. In addition, discomforts such as a toothache are often somewhat relieved because the pain threshold rises.

Over thousands of years, people have developed a tremendous number of cultural habits and rituals around food and eating. To eat with someone is to establish a connection, or at least make a connection possible. A business dinner is a signal that the participants are not to be thought of as enemies but as friends between whom a deal can be made—and the result of the meal is often a signed contract.

When a man and a woman in the early stages of becoming acquainted decide to go out to dinner, they are seldom most interested in the food. Instead, the meal functions as a preliminary way of exploring and deepening the relationship. Perhaps they can even fantasize about the possibility of a sexual connection if everything else clicks in this contact between them. This possibility of bonding through eating together may have given rise to the saying that the way to a man's heart is through his stomach.

Even the Christian sacrament of Holy Communion can be said to be a ritualized expression of closeness and the elimination of boundaries in connection with a meal. After administering the bread and wine, the clergyperson declares that the communicants are now one with the body and blood of Christ. Similar ritual meals are found in other religions.

As many of us know, food is also used to achieve a sense of well-being even if we do not actually need to eat, and fatty foods comfort us more than low-fat or protein-rich foods. When we feel anxious and cannot sleep, we get up and have a midnight snack and a glass of milk. Warm milk especially seems to be relaxing.

When young people go away to college or leave home for some other reason, it is not unusual for them to gain weight, perhaps as a result of eating themselves out of their feelings of homesickness. To long for home is to long for closeness and familiar contact. The loss of that closeness creates an anxiety that we try to deaden with food, often without being conscious of what we are doing. When we try to lose weight by reducing the amount of fat in our diets, the same thing happens. Some people become anxious and depressed, while others become more active and upbeat. The pattern we exhibit appears to be inborn or at least imprinted on us very early in life.

Eating Disorders

We all have our personal histories, but for most of us, feelings of anxiety, uneasiness, and loneliness can be relieved with food. People may let us down and not live up to our expectations, but food is dependable and, at least in more fortunate societies, always there. Food can in this way begin to function as a substitute for both closeness and love. It is as if hunger for friends becomes hunger for food.

Having a midnight snack every so often is not harmful, but a behavioral pattern of regularly deadening anxiety, depression, or other negative feelings with food can in the long run cause eating disorders. It appears that some people have an innate susceptibility to these disorders, while others can abuse food to a degree without risking the loss of control that characterizes bulimia and anorexia. Psychological factors also play an important role as a cause of eating disorders, to say nothing of the pictures of wafer-thin models that make young girls dissatisfied with their bodies.

All extremes in the way we eat have negative consequences in the long run. Excessive weight is hard to lose and increases the strain on other parts of the body, such as the joints and the cardiovascular system. When we diet excessively, on the other hand, the body reacts by going into starvation mode and, instead of dropping weight, increases the effectiveness of its nutritional storage. This is why some people say they get fatter just by looking at a piece of cake. Their metabolism has become more efficient, so they store more nutrients when they eat something. Another effect of dieting is a vicious cycle: Voluntary starvation often leads to anxiety and strain that must be dealt with one way or another, often by once again deadening negative emotions with food.

Bingeing and purging cause one's metabolism, along with emotional moods, to swing from one extreme to the other. As overeating induces the body to become more efficient in handling nutrients, some people, especially young women, try to counter the weight gain by vomiting up their food or by exercising compulsively. It is hard to imagine the anxiety and apprehension that people suffering from anorexia or bulimia must endure. An eating disorder causes life-threatening behavior. Sufferers perceive their behavior as evil and thus develop a poor self-image and feelings of fear and shame.

The connection between oxytocin and overeating, bulimia, and anorexia is still unclear. Since oxytocin plays an important role in the body's system for registering fullness, and for mental and physical relaxation, it may prove useful in the treatment of eating disorders. It is to be hoped that research will in time lead to the development of new ways to help those afflicted by this dangerous distortion of one of life's basic needs and pleasures.

❧ 15

Cigarettes, Alcohol, and Other Drugs

Human beings have developed various techniques for alleviating the stress and strain that have always been part of our lives. As we saw in the previous chapter, the feeling of a full stomach generates peace and calm, an effect that has led not only to gourmet cooking but also to obesity and eating disorders. For many people, another route with mixed consequences is the use of nicotine and alcohol.

For the smoker, a cigarette provides comfort, relaxation, and heightened concentration. It may be the dot over the "i" after a good meal. Smoking works in many relatively unrecognized ways. Nicotine depresses the appetite and increases the burning of ingested calories; that is why people usually gain weight when they stop smoking. Thus many people, particularly women, continue smoking despite warnings about its risks.

Smoking also involves something else more directly connected with the subject of this book. Many people have noted the similarity between sucking on a thumb and sucking on a cigarette. Smoking activates the same types of effects found in a small child's sucking on a nipple or a thumb. Nipple sucking and probably smoking release oxytocin and activate the gastrointestinal hormone system. Smoking thus may produce a feeling of comfort in much the same way as thumb-sucking does. In the psychoanalytic model, smoking could be a return to the oral stage of development, corresponding to the earliest part of life in which sucking and fullness are central to well-being. Since we know how important oxytocin is during this phase of development, I believe that both explanations reinforce rather than contradict each other.

There are also other typical oxytocin-related elements in smoking. Anyone who has been a smoker knows how strong the bond with cigarettes is. You don't go anywhere without your smokes and your matches, and if you forget them, you feel lost. In addition, a connection develops between smokers that cannot be explained just by the social interchange that takes place in the smoking room. If we smoke, we have something in common with other smokers. While we suck away on our cigarettes, cigars, or pipes, we inhale not only nicotine (and the other poisonous substances in tobacco smoke), but we probably also trigger, through the sucking and the social contact, a release of oxytocin that makes us inclined to see the other smokers around us as our friends (in contrast to the unsympathetic nonsmokers who want nothing more than to box smokers in with prohibitions). Rituals that develop around smoking often promote contact between smokers—for example, borrowing cigarettes from each other, the subtle intimacy of lighting a cigarette for someone, or giving a carton of cigarettes as a present from the duty-free shop after a trip abroad. People who have been regular smokers most likely recognize themselves in the above description.

One paradoxical effect of smoking is that it decreases oxytocin in nursing mothers, and, as a result, these mothers produce less milk. Another interesting effect of smoking is the release of vasopressin. It is possible that vasopressin promotes the increased concentration and burning of calories associated with smoking.

A Drink to Unwind

In our culture, we use alcohol more or less liberally, often with the objective of reducing our nervousness and anxiety in social situations. Sometimes a drinking habit reaches the point of alcohol abuse, but a moderate use of alcohol in connection with anxiety reduction is not only culturally acceptable but effective.

At a party or some other occasion where many new faces are present, a drink under the belt as well as one in the hand makes it easier to approach and talk to strangers. One classic scene is the old barn dance, where a young lad took a swig or two from a pocket flask to get up enough courage to ask a girl to dance—a scene that has now shifted to the discotheques and clubs.

Many people also use alcohol to unwind after a busy day. Even if you are home only for a quick change of clothes before going out for the evening, a drink can put you in the right mood and make the day's stress and worries fade into the background for a while; you can then enjoy being sociable or even flirtatious and open to new relationships.

Experiments with both rats and human subjects show that moderate amounts of alcohol increase the concentration of oxytocin in the blood. (Higher amounts of alcohol, however, have the opposite effect.) Therefore, the calming effect of a moderate amount of alcohol may be caused at least in part by oxytocin. When rats were given a small amount of alcohol, their tolerance for pain increased, but when they were then injected with an oxytocin antagonist, this heightened pain threshold disappeared.

The classic oxytocin effect that facilitates the flow of breast milk is strengthened by alcohol (though for other reasons it may be inadvisable to drink alcohol while nursing). This connection is behind the old custom of giving a glass of beer to a woman who is having trouble nursing her baby. Even today, nursing mothers discuss the pros and cons of drinking beer in that context. Unfortunately, it is the alcohol in beer, rather than any other ingredient, that facilitates nursing.

Research in recent years has revised many of our conceptions about alcohol. Among other things, a moderate consumption of alcohol, especially red wine, appears to be correlated with a lower incidence of cardiovascular illnesses. This effect may be related directly to specific substances, particularly bioflavonoids (naturally occurring flavor compounds found in many fruits and vegetables and in red wine), but the oxytocin that is released under the influence of alcohol may also play a significant role.

Other Drugs

Narcotic drugs, such as morphine and heroin, have long been used to escape stress and anxiety, though with greater physiological (and legal) risks than alcohol. Results from some recent animal studies indicate that oxytocin may play a dual role in drug dependency. These experiments have involved the administration of morphine and cocaine (and alcohol, as discussed above). It is difficult to interpret the results of this research; it implies that oxytocin may be involved in the physiological process that leads to development of a drug dependency, and yet that high levels of oxytocin might have a preventive effect. Cocaine's effects are connected with higher activity related to the neurotransmitter dopamine, and oxytocin influences dopamine.

A few studies have begun to illuminate the links between marijuana use and oxytocin. Some have shown that marijuana may stimulate the release of oxytocin to produce calm and ease social encounters. Other studies of the use of lithium (used in psychiatric medicine) to reduce symptoms of withdrawal from marijuana use have shown that lithium's effect is linked with activation of oxytocin-releasing nerve cells.

The still unclear connections between oxytocin and narcotic drugs offer fertile grounds for more research.

16

Medication-Induced Calm and Connection

Certain medicines used today have positive effects because they most likely stimulate the calm and connection system indirectly by promoting the body's release of oxytocin.

As discussed in Chapter 5, oxytocin interacts with different chemical signal systems that function as message bearers in the nervous system. Serotonin, dopamine, and noradrenaline, some of the brain's important signaling substances, regulate different body functions and also influence the release of oxytocin in one way or another. Oxytocin in its turn most likely influences the release and activity of these signaling substances.

Drugs for Anxiety, Depression, and Psychosis

Some of the medications used in the treatment of anxiety and depression affect the activity of the serotonin system. They include, for example, substances that activate certain serotonin receptors (5HT 1a) as well as the current popular and widely used selective serotonin reuptake inhibitors (SSRIs), in common parlance often called Prozac after the most well-known product of this sort prescribed in the United States. Low levels of serotonin are related to depression and certain types of anxiety; for this reason, medications such as Prozac are believed to work by raising the level of serotonin.

Even people who do not actually have these symptoms can become more sociable if they take SSRI drugs. Since research on rats shows that elevated levels of serotonin cause the release of oxytocin, and SSRI medications raise the serotonin level, some of the effect of those medicines can indeed be caused by activation of the patient's oxytocin system. Other research results support my theory that oxytocin plays a role in the effects of SSRI drugs. In a study of people with obsessive-compulsive disorders, oxytocin levels rose in patients who improved with the medication, but did not go up in those who were not helped by the treatment.

Certain animal experiments have also been constructed to mirror depression in humans, and here also oxytocin has shown itself effective in counteracting the rats' "depression." Oxytocin has not yet been administered to people suffering from depression; however, a connection is shown through the fact that patients who do suffer from this illness have uncommonly low levels of oxytocin.

It is fortunate that antidepressive medications are available, since they help many people live normally and avoid long-term disability. But all drugs have side effects, and many of the side effects of SSRIs are serious.

Can we then conclude that oxytocin would be a good medication for treating anxiety and depression? There is definitely support for such an idea. As I have already shown, rats that are treated with oxytocin not only become calmer and less fearful but also increase their social contacts. Breast-feeding women, who have high oxytocin levels in their blood during the entire nursing period, display calmer behavior and greater interest in social interchange with close family and friends than women who do not nurse. Even women who before pregnancy had symptoms of anxiety and obsessive-compulsive disorders often experience a reduction of these symptoms during nursing, an effect that probably has no other explanation than the increased oxytocin secretion during that period. (We must not forget, however, that there are some women who, because of their individual psychophysiological or environmental circumstances, suffer increased anxiety and depression during the period of nursing.)

Reduced agitation and increased sociability are related, as we know, with high oxytocin levels. Therefore, it is important to contemplate further which medical benefits might result from a wider use of oxytocin in medicinal form in the future.

Barriers to the Use of Oxytocin As a Medication

Despite its beneficial influence, oxytocin is not generally used as a medication today; it is used primarily in childbirth. Pitocin, an oxytocin solution, is used to produce contractions in the muscles of the uterus, either to induce labor or to strengthen the effectiveness of the contractions when the delivery is underway. An intravenous drip of oxytocin can also facilitate the expulsion of the placenta after the baby is born. Another medicinal application of the substance is through a nasal spray, used to stimulate milk expulsion in women who have difficulty nursing.

Beyond this, oxytocin is not administered through medications at the present time because it poses various pharmacological problems. One difficulty is that, because the substance breaks down quickly in the gastrointestinal system, it is not very successful as a form of medicine that is swallowed. The only way to administer oxytocin with noticeable effect is through injection. Unfortunately, this method is not especially user-friendly, and the substance breaks down rapidly in the bloodstream as well. It is also difficult for oxytocin to reach the brain because of the so-called blood-brain barrier created by the dense walls of the brain's blood vessels to prevent dangerous substances from penetrating this vital organ.

To develop effective medicinal applications of oxytocin, we must make the oxytocin molecule easier to handle. Chemical techniques for doing this exist today, but they are still not commercially viable. It may also be possible to create oxytocin-like drugs that would produce specific isolated effects of oxytocin, such as stress relief, pain alleviation, calming effects, healing, or growth enhancement, since these appear to be linked to different parts of the oxytocin molecule.

The same reasoning carries over to other medications. Several drugs used in the treatment of schizophrenia might also involve the patient's natural oxytocin. The classic schizophrenia medicines are thought to function by blocking the effect of dopamine on the dopamine receptors in the central nervous system. Another group of medications used for the same disease, the so-called atypical neuroleptics, includes Clozapin and Amperozid. The mechanism by which these preparations work is not clearly understood, but, interestingly, patients who are treated with them generally become more open to increased contact with the people around them. Not surprisingly, these drugs promote the release of oxytocin in animals. The patients' improved social skills and interest in their surroundings are probably to some degree a result of increased oxytocin activity.

Treating Symptoms of Stress

A common element in a large group of illnesses is an apparent connection to recent or past stress. Patients with such illnesses exhibit not only mental symptoms such as anxiety and depression, but also physical symptoms of tiredness and diffuse poor health. They also often have specific aches and pains that have no real physical explanation. Typically, it is difficult to find an effective remedy for these symptoms in current pharmacology.

For example, fibromyalgia is difficult to cure, and its sufferers, mostly women, are plagued by tiredness and pain.

Fibromyalgia is now thought to be a type of reaction to stress. Because oxytocin provides calming and pain-reducing effects, it should theoretically be useful in the treatment of fibromyalgia patients. Not surprisingly, many of them improve with massage. As an additional sign that oxytocin is involved, fibromyalgic women with low oxytocin levels exhibit more symptoms of stress, depression, and pain than do those with higher oxytocin levels. Conversely, the more such women report a feeling of well-being and happiness, the higher their oxytocin levels are.

Children who suffer chronic stomach-aches usually have lower oxytocin levels than children of the same age without that problem, so perhaps colic would be reduced if oxytocin levels could be raised. Even certain psychosomatic stomach problems in adults have been connected with low levels of oxytocin.

Other conditions characterized by defensive reactions should theoretically respond to treatment with oxytocin. One example is children diagnosed with attention deficit and hyperactivity disorder (ADHD). Since oxytocin can induce calm and enhance learning, perhaps these problems could be treated more beneficially with oxytocin than with the drugs (such as Ritalin) used today. High blood pressure is another candidate for some type of oxytocin medication.

I also believe that oxytocin might be given to people for preventive purposes, such as to counter the effects of stress early in life. It is now apparent that children can be stressed even in the womb. One sign of this is that they have a low birth weight even if they are born at full term. These children have an increased risk of stress-related illnesses, such as cardiovascular disease, as adults.

Young rats that get too little nourishment in utero do not grow as well later in life as other rats. They also have abnormally high levels of stress hormones as adults. As mentioned earlier, oxytocin injections given to young rats days after birth can somehow cancel out these effects.

What would happen if newborn babies received oxytocin or calming massage to counteract the negative effects of the stress experienced in utero, during birth, and in the first days of life? Would their growth and future stress levels be influenced in a positive way?

For the time being, these possibilities do not exist, either in pharmacology or in medical policy. Although levels of oxytocin can be increased in natural ways, we must bide our time and await the day when the oxytocin molecule is able to be administered directly, allowing us to take greater advantage of its positive effects.

More important, by learning to use massage and other techniques that release the body's own oxytocin, we could perhaps raise the body's oxytocin levels in a way that gives people the possibility of enjoying its healthful effects without the need to take a pill or injection. We have this wonderful healing substance inside us and need only to learn the many ways we can draw upon it.

Motion and Stillness

As we have seen, our minds and bodies are constantly striving for balance, even if we are not always conscious of it. We need balance between rest and activity, between calm and exertion. One of the activities that helps us achieve this balance is exercise. Running in the woods, sweating through a workout at the gym, or exercising in some other way generally does the body good (if you don't overdo it, of course).

Exercise has short-term and long-term beneficial effects. After a workout, you feel satisfied, pleased with yourself, and often quite refreshed, and in the long run you also become stronger and healthier. Perhaps you exercise to get into shape, develop more stamina, or keep off excess pounds. Or you might be one of those people who need to exercise regularly in order to feel really good. No matter what reason you have for running, walking, or going to the gym, you benefit from your exercise more or less consciously in many ways. Your lung capacity increases, you burn stored calories, you have a better appetite, and you become physically stronger. But you also become mentally calmer and feel better in general. Since your blood pressure goes down with exercise, as do levels of stress hormones, there is reason to believe that exercise in some way activates the calm and connection system and releases oxytocin in the body.

As expected, animal studies support this assertion. Researchers have bred a certain type of rat that has higher than average blood pressure. If such rats are exercised on a rotating wheel, their blood pressure falls, and they become less aggressive. But if they are then prevented from exercising in this way, their blood pressure rises and their aggressiveness returns. This result has been interpreted to demonstrate that the exercise on the wheel releases endorphins, opiates produced within the body, that have an effect similar to that of morphine.

It is not certain, however, that this is the whole story. Oxytocin levels also rise in these exercising rats. Does this mean that the act of moving triggers the release of oxytocin under certain conditions? We do know that the activation of sensory nerve fibers in the muscles and joints (something that happens when we exercise) causes the release of oxytocin in the brain. We also know that oxytocin injections increase the production of certain endorphins, indicating a connection between the two systems. The pain-relieving action of oxytocin, both short-term and long-term, is mediated via endorphins. If exercise releases oxytocin, and if that substance promotes the release of endorphins, then oxytocin may be one of the physiological links between exercise and endorphins.

Another reason to presume a connection between oxytocin and endorphins is that the pain-reducing effect of acupuncture does not materialize if an oxytocin antagonist is given at the same time. Since we know that acupuncture works via the endorphin system, this discovery also implies a connection between the two biochemical systems. Future research will most likely clarify how the systems work together and in parallel.

As I see it, exercise is just one of several different ways of activating the calm and connection system. The system can be reached via nerves from the skin, the mammary glands, the interior of the gastrointestinal organs, and the muscles. We tend to choose different ways of accessing this system during different periods of life. When we are young, we are more likely to generate oxytocin through exercise, but as we age, we may opt for acupuncture or massage. We are in a state of constant feedback with our environment, and we need activating as well as calming stimuli to be in balance. Perhaps the reason a hamster stops running on a wheel when she has her young and then takes up the habit nearly immediately after the babies are weaned is that her calm and connection system is being stimulated by both activities.

Thus the increased supply of both oxytocin and endorphins is probably the reason why we feel good, calm, and even happy when we regularly run or work out at the gym. The healthful physiological effects of exercise that directly fit the oxytocin profile include lower blood pressure, lower levels of stress hormone, lower pulse rate, and more effective digestion. Just as these effects become more pronounced if laboratory animals receive several oxytocin injections over time, repeated exercise has a greater and more lasting effect on our bodies.

Sedentary Jogging

Not everyone likes to run. Some people would rather spend their time in quiet activities. Fortunately, there are also many mental techniques that help us attain calm and relaxation, and most of them probably also activate the antistress branch of the oxytocin tree.

Yoga in its various forms is one example of the many Eastern methods of seeking balance. Over thousands of years, the tradition of yoga has developed many experience-based techniques to promote health and long life. There is certainly a connection between yoga's different body positions and breathing techniques and the release of the body's natural oxytocin. Yoga movements stimulate physical locations (the groin, the front of the body) that have a strong link to the activation of the vagal nerve system through connected touch receptors.

Meditation, sometimes connected with yoga, is another method for stilling thoughts and achieving both physical and psychological relaxation. Most often a purely mental technique without body movement, meditation is gaining wide acceptance in Western cultures. In many meditation techniques, it is customary for a person to focus on a monotonous stimulus such as a mantra, one or more words of known or unknown meaning that are repeated silently, as a way to still the activity of thinking. Some meditations require the lengthy contemplation of an object, such as a candle flame; others concentrate on the calm rhythm of breathing. Some forms of meditation are done while walking, again with an emphasis on breathing and a steady rhythm.

The repetition of words or rhythms is a method that has been used cross-culturally throughout the ages to create a state of trance. This technique is as much involved in the Catholic's repetition of the Ave Maria as it is in the African's drum rhythm. Certain interesting similarities exist between these rhythmic ritualistic patterns and the activation of the oxytocin system through the light stroking of rats (as in the experiment described in Chapter 9). In both examples, the stimulation happens slowly and with a regular rhythm. A frequency of forty strokes per minute gave optimal results in the rat experiment. Perhaps there is also an optimal frequency for the repetition of a mantra or a shaman's drum rhythm. Stroking, massage, and loud drum beats involve repeated physical stimuli, but meditation invokes mental pictures and words to achieve the effect.

Meditative techniques lead us to reduce the amount of attention focused outward and instead to turn our attention inward and become more open to our mental and emotional processes. We might say that relaxation and trance techniques involve a reduction of activity in the left brain and an increase in activity in the right brain. After long practice, one can become more adept at achieving a state of inner clarity and peace. According to some researchers, long-term meditation can also cause the right brain, considered to be the site for more intuitive, feeling-related, and comprehensive thinking, to have a greater influence on an individual's thought processes. This may happen as both halves of the brain in some way become better synchronized with each other.

The physiological effects of meditation have been closely studied. We know that it generally produces decreased oxygen consumption, lower pulse and breath rates, and relaxed muscles. A decrease in perspiration leads to a reduction in the skin's conductivity of a weak electric current. All these effects can be interpreted as the result of reduced activity in the sympathetic nervous system. In addition, a change in the pattern of brain activity can be seen on an electroencephalogram (EEG), which shows among other things an increase in the long alpha waves associated with deep sleep.

Regular meditation can lower blood pressure in a person with hypertension and help normalize the heartbeat. Stress hormone levels fall, and the experience of pain becomes less pronounced. There are even indications that a meditation regimen can reduce or eliminate abusive habits such as excessive alcohol consumption or smoking.

We can all observe for ourselves the connection between the rhythm of the breath and the frequency of the heartbeat. Inhaling increases the pulse through activation of the sympathetic nervous system; exhaling produces relaxation, reduces the pulse rate, and activates the vagus nerve in the autonomic nervous system. Various methods for biofeedback, relaxation, and healing are based on breathing techniques. We do not know exactly which physiological reactions these techniques evoke. Perhaps the effect of breath therapies depends in part on the increased supply of oxygen in the blood obtained through rapid breathing, and in part on the alternating tensing and relaxing movement of the lung muscles that activates sensory nerves to send signals via the vagus nerve to the calm and connection system.

Hypnosis is another method for producing a state of deep rest and relaxation. This state is achieved in part by simulating pleasant experiences in the mind through conjuring up imaginary pictures and feelings. Sometimes reduced skin conductivity has been measured in people under hypnosis. As in meditation, this can be related to decreased activity in the sympathetic nervous system and increased activity in the parasympathetic nervous system.

Meditation, hypnosis, techniques of touch, and methods for relaxation all have in common a profile of effects that is reminiscent of the effects of oxytocin. Even though the connection between meditation and the oxytocin system is based so far on circumstantial evidence, the similarities in the pattern of effects are striking.

In addition to the mental techniques discussed above, we must also mention a large group of therapies used in what is known as alternative, or complementary, medicine. The effects of these therapies are thought to be produced not via the nervous system or the blood, but through a third physiological communication system, the so-called meridian system. Chinese medicine, including acupuncture, acupressure, and similar techniques, belongs in this category.

It lies outside the scope of this book to try to describe or explain the meridian system. But it appears that acupuncture might operate through the release of oxytocin. As mentioned, my experiments with my colleagues have shown that acupuncture's pain-alleviating effect is counteracted if the animals are also treated with an oxytocin antagonist. It is also possible that the long-term calming effects of acupuncture could be connected with oxytocin, but that has not yet been experimentally tested.

Even mental images, such as those called up through hypnosis, appear to elicit effects that resemble those of oxytocin. This is one way in which what we think about can have physiological significance for our well-being. Perhaps this is the seed of a scientific explanation for why "positive thinking" has long been a popular form of therapy, both in the area of personal development and in alternative medical treatments. Though we can't simply "think ourselves healthy," we can help the healing process with our minds. Positive, light, and happy thoughts probably activate the oxytocin system, which in turn has a healthy effect on our entire physiology and psychology. Many people have experienced the opposite: Gloomy or pessimistic thoughts can lead to a vicious cycle of depression that is accompanied by the physiological dimensions that medical science is now beginning to identify. Inner images probably do not even need to be conscious to influence us, because repressed memories can also affect our inner balance and physiological reactions.

Many people say that the best meditation is a run outside in the wonder of nature. This is far from a foolish notion, especially since it highlights the common ground between meditation and physical activity. Both give us badly needed, deeply desired calm. Both make us peaceful and open to others. Prayer, close contact with nature, and certain music can all lull us into a state of relaxation and peace.

There are thus many roads to calm and connection. The ways we choose depend on our culture, traditions, environment, life circumstances, available options, and individual preferences. But in response to the common need for calm, healing, and deep repose, we have an innate ability to activate a system within our bodies that will help us to attain this state.

~ 18

Our Inner Ecology

At the beginning of this book, I explained that because we have concentrated almost exclusively on the fight or flight response to challenges in our environment, historically there has been an imbalance in our knowledge of physiology. The information in these chapters is my attempt to begin to correct this imbalance by describing some of what has been discovered so far about the complementary system of calm and connection. I have also moved beyond our current scientific knowledge to speculate about various activities and techniques in which oxytocin's effects seem to be operative, even if they have not yet been documented. If we can explore these techniques and consciously choose to incorporate their positive effects into our lives, we can increase our chances to live in a state of health and well-being.

The calm and connection system, as we have seen, has a balancing effect on physiology in humans and animals. Oxytocin lowers the blood pressure and pulse rate, keeps the bloodstream from being flooded with stress hormones, and helps the body handle food in an optimal way. This natural healing nectar provides an antidote to the negative effects of a fast-paced lifestyle marked by the stress and anxiety that come with competition. Even if we habitually overload the side of the see-saw that involves stress and activity, we fortunately have a chance to counteract some of the resulting negative effects by periodically putting emphasis on the antistress side to an equivalent degree.

We can consciously stimulate our calm and connection systems without negative side effects by choosing from various methods, both old and new, that are served up in the oxytocin smorgasbord. When we get a massage, and probably when we get an acupuncture treatment, oxytocin is released in our bodies. When we exercise, make love, meditate, or spend time with people we like, when we are having fun and enjoying life, this substance is working in our bodies. There are also less healthy ways to release oxytocin. Alcohol, mood-altering drugs, and fatty foods certainly give us higher oxytocin levels; but sooner or later, most of us have negative consequences from these routes to calm. We need to make informed choices.

It is possible that women, due to their physiology and traditional life experiences, find it somewhat easier than men to reach and recognize the state of calm and connection. For this reason, it is all the more fortunate that female researchers have now entered the formerly male-dominated world of biomedicine. We know that the male sex hormone testosterone increases the release of vasopressin, and that these biochemicals have a "natural" connection with physical activity, aggressiveness, and defense. We also know that the female sex hormone estrogen functions as an oxytocin enhancer, which can make women more inclined toward activities that promote calm and connection. But it is important to recognize that both sexes secrete these hormones, that both sexes have access to and need for the calm and connection system as well as the fight or flight reaction, and that individual differences between and among women and men have causes that can outweigh all stereotyped "anatomy is destiny" effects.

Ever since research discovered and described the fight or flight reaction, it has been clear that this physiological system is vital to survival, to the ability to mobilize our resources and perform at our highest levels, at least for a short time. When we look at society today, however, it seems that the fight or flight attributes have become the sole basis for many values and standards about how people should live. Independence, competition, efficiency, achievement, and power are highly valued.

However, we are equally adapted biologically for living in a very different way. We are intrinsically structured to be able to connect, nurture, rest, reflect, and rejoice. We are made to love and to experience sexual ecstasy with a partner. We have the innate ability to feed our bodies, minds, and spirits, both literally and figuratively, and to take pleasure in what they can do. We are created with the need and the means to enjoy life without guilt or shame. And it is time for us to acknowledge that the psychophysiology of these innate human capacities is equally essential for our health and ultimate survival.

Today's stressful lifestyles strike down too many people, at younger and younger ages, with burnout and ill health, both physical and mental. Many of the illnesses suffered by people of all ages are ultimately caused by stress. Both we and the society we live in have a crying need for something different—and that something different is nearer than we might think. We actually have the key within us, in the potential for evoking calm and connection through the working of a biological system that until now has been hidden in the shadow of the all-too-familiar fight or flight system.

Nature incorporates an overall pattern of relationships, which we call ecology, that must be balanced if flora and fauna are to establish a sustainable system. For the ecological balance not to be disturbed, the system must be able to handle activities and resources in such a way that no irreversible harm occurs.

We humans must begin to think of our health and well-being as our own inner ecology. Our bodies will not continue to work well if we constantly overexert them and exploit their resources. We need to replenish our empty stores, regain our strength, rest, and heal. We have known this for a long time, of course, but only now are we beginning to understand the physiological processes involved and the ways we can consciously choose to activate them. If we really understand how we function physiologically, we may become part of a shift, both individual and cultural, away from the stress-oriented imbalance of modern society.

Today, drugs that raise the serotonin level and, as we have seen, the oxytocin level as well are the most popular medicines in the Western world. Even people who could be considered healthy are taking such preparations to become less fearful, happier, and more optimistic.

But we have other alternatives. We can choose activities and pursuits that release the oxytocin stored in our own inner medicine cabinet. With this vital knowledge about the calm and connection system, we can choose to make exercise, meditation, or massage a priority over extra hours at work. We can choose to lie down for a short rest before running out to buy groceries. We can play with our children or take a walk instead of scheduling power breakfasts or spending hours at the computer.

What changes these choices might lead to in the long run I can only speculate about. In this we are all unique. But my hope is that we will all learn to listen to what the workings of oxytocin and the calm and connection system are trying to say to us.

Life does not have to be only a struggle. It can and should also be a dance among the roses.

References

Chapter 3: An Essential Balance

Folow, B. Physiological aspects of the defense and defeat reactions. *Acta Physiologica Scandinavica* 1997:161, 34–37.

Uvnäs Wallensten, K., and J. Järhult. Reflex activation of the sympatho-adrenal system inhibits the gastrin release caused by electrical vagal stimulation in cats. *Acta Physiologica Scandinavica* 1982:114, 297–302.

Uvnäs Moberg, K. Release of gastrointestinal peptides in response to vagal activation induced by electrical stimulation, feeding and suckling. *Journal of the Autonomic Nervous System* 1983:9, 141–155.

————. Oxytocin-linked antistress effects—the relaxation and growth response. *Acta Physiologica Scandinavica* 1997:161 (suppl 640) 38–42.

————. Antistress pattern induced by oxytocin. *News in Physiological Sciences* 1998:13, 22–26.

Chapter 4: The Body's Control Centers

Eriksson M., et al. Distribution and origin of peptide containing nerve fibers in the rat and human mammary gland. *Neuroscience Letters* 1996:1, 227–245.

Guyton, A. *Textbook of medical physiology*. Chap. 8: 45–61, 74–83. W. B. Saunders Company, 1991.

Johansson, R. S., et al. Mechanoreceptor activity from the human face and oral mucosa. *Experimental Brain Research* 1998: 204–208.

Komisaruk, B. R., et al. Brain-mediated responses to vaginocervical stimulation in spinal cord-transected rats: Role of the vagus nerves. *Brain Research Bulletin* 1996:708, 128–134.

Olausson, H., Y. Lamarre, H. Backlund, C. Morin, B. G. Wallin, G. Starck, S. Ekholm, I. Strigo, K. Worsley, Å. B. Vallbo, and M. C. Bushnell. Unmyelinated tactile afferents signal touch and project to insular cortex. *Nature* 2002:5, 900–904.

Vallbo, Å., et al. A system of unmyelinated afferents for innocuous mechanorecption in the human skin. *Brain Research Bulletin* 1993: 628, 301–304.

Chapter 5: How Oxytocin Works

For an overview of the functions of oxytocin, see:

Argiolas A., and G. L. Gess. Central functions of oxytocin. *Neuroscience Biobehavioural Reviews* 1991:15, 217–231.

Petersson, M. Short- and long-term cardiovascular and behavioural effects of oxytocin—mechanisms involved and influence of female steroid hormones. Stockholm: Dissertation, Karolinska Institute 1999.

Original research papers:

Archer, A., J. Chauvet, and M. T. Chauvet. Man and the chimaera: Selective versus neutral oxytocin evolution. I: *Oxytocin: Cellular and molecular approaches in medicine and research* (eds.: R. Ivell and J. A. Russel). New York: Plenum Press, 1995: 615–627.

Dale, H. H. On some physiological actions of ergot. *Journal of physiology* 1906:34, 163–206.

Kimura, T. Investigation of the oxytocin receptor at the molecular level. I: *Oxytocin: Cellular and Molecular Approaches in Medicine and Research* (eds.: R. Ivell and A. J. Russel). New York: Plenum Press 1995: 259–268.

Ostrowsky, N. L. Oxytocin receptor mRNA expression in rat brain: Implications for behavioural integration and reproductive success. *Psychoneuroendocrinology* 1988:23, 989–1004.

Ott, I., and J. C. Scott. The action of infundibilin upon the mammary secretion. *Proceedings of the Society for Experimental Biology and Medicine* 1910:8, 137–142.

Sofroniew, M. W. Vasopressin and oxytocin in mammalian brain and spinal cord. *Trends in Neurosciences* 1983:6, 467–472.

Wakerley, J. B., and C. D. Ingram. Synchronization of bursting in hypothalamic oxytocin neurons: Possible coordinating mechanisms. *New in Physiological Sciences* 1993:8, 129–133.

Chapter 6: Effects of Oxytocin Injections

For an overview of oxytocin's effects see:

Richard, P., F. Moos, and M. J. Freund-Mercier. Central effects of oxytocin. *Physiological Reviews* 1991:71, 331–370.

Uvnäs Moberg, K. Antistress pattern induced by oxytocin. *News in Physiological Sciences* (NIPS) 1998:27, 22–26.

Original research papers:

Diaz-Cabiale Z., et al. Oxytocin/alfa2-receptor interactions on feeding responses. *Neuroendocrinology* 2000.

Petersson, M., et al. Oxytocin increases nociceptive thresholds in a long-term perspective in female and male rats. *Neuroscience Letters* 1966:212, 87–90.

Petersson, M., et al. Oxytocin causes a long-term decrease of blood pressure in female and male rats. *Physiology & Behaviour* 1996:60, 5, 1311–1315.

Petersson, M., et al. Steroid dependent effects of oxytocin on spontaneous motor activity in female rats. *Brain Research Bulletin* 1998:19, 301–305.

Petersson, M., et al. Oxytocin increases locus coeruleus alpha2-adrenoreceptor responsiveness in rats. *Neuroscience Letters* 1998:255, 115–118.

Petersson, M., A. L. Hulting, and K. Uvnäs Moberg. Oxytocin causes a sustained decrease in plasma levels of corticosterone in rats. *Neuroscience Letters* 1999: 264, 41–44.

Petersson M., T. Lundeberg, and K. Uvnäs Moberg. Short-term increase and long-term decrease of blood pressure in response to oxytocin—potentiating effect of female steroid hormones. *Journal of Cardiovascular Pharmacology* 1999:33, 10–108.

_____. Oxytocin enhances the effects of clonidine on blood pressure and locomoter activity in rats. *Journal of the Autonomic Nervous System* 1999:78, 49–56.

Uvnäs Moberg, K., et al. High doses of oxytocin cause sedation and low doses cause an anxiolytic-like effect in male rats. *Pharmacology, Biochemistry & Behaviour* 1994:49, 101–106.

Uvnäs Moberg, K., et al. Endocrine and behavioural traits in low-avoidance Sprague-Dawley rats. *Regulatory Peptides* 1999:80, 75–82.

Uvnäs Moberg, K., et al. Improved conditioned avoidance learning by oxytocin administration in high emotional, but not low emotional Sprague-Dawley rats. *Regulatory Peptides* 2000.

Chapter 7: The Oxytocin Tree

Björkstrand, E., M. Eriksson, and K, Uvnäs Moberg. Evidence of a peripheral and a central effect of oxytocin on pancreatic hormone release in rats. *Neuroendocrinology* 1996:63, 377–383.

Björkstrand E., A. L. Hulting, and K. Uvnäs Moberg. Evidence for a dual function of oxytocin in the control of growth hormone secretion. *Regulatory Peptides* 1997:69, 1–5.

Björkstrand, E., and K. Uvnäs Moberg. Central oxytocin increases food intake and daily weight gain in rats. *Physiology and Behaviour* 1996:59, 947–952.

Furuya, K., et al. A novel biological aspect of ovarian oxytocin: Gene expression of oxytocin and oxytocin receptor in cumulus/luteal cells and the effect of oxytocin on embryogenesis in fertilized oocytes. *Advances in Experimental Medical Biology* 1995:395, 523–528.

Lederis, K., H. J. Goren, and M. D. Hollenbergh. Oxytocin: An insulin-like hormone. I: *Oxytocin: Clinical and Laboratory Studies* (eds.: J. A. Amico and F. Robinson). Amsterdam: Elsevier Science Publishers, 1985, 53–76.

Petersson, M., et al. Oxytocin increases the survival of musculocutaneous flaps. *Naunyn-Schmiedeberg's Archives of Pharmacology* 1998:357, 701–704.

Sohlström, A., et al. Effects of oxytocin treatment early in pregnancy, on fetal growth, in ad libitum fed and food restricted rats. *Pediatric Research* 1999:46, 339–344.

Uvnäs Moberg, K., P. Alster, and M. Petersson. Dissociation of oxytocin effects on body weight in two variants of female Sprague-Dawley rats. *Integrative Physiology and Behavioural Sciences* 1996:31, 44–55.

Uvnäs Moberg, K., et al. Postnatal oxytocin injections cause sustained weight gain and increased nociceptive thresholds in male and female rats. *Pediatric Research* 1998:43, 1–5.

Chapter 8: Nursing: Oxytocin's Starring Role

Altemus, M., et al. Suppression of hypothalamic pituitary adrenal axis responses to stress in lactating women. *Journal of Clinical Endocrinology and Metabolism* 1995:80, 2954–2959.

Eriksson, M., T. Lundeberg, and K. Uvnäs Moberg. Studies on cutaneous blood flow in the mammary gland of lactating rats. *Acta Physiologica Scandinavica* 1996:158, 1–6.

Johansson, B., K. Svennersten-Sjaunja, and K. Uvnäs Moberg. Coordinating role of oxytocin on milking-related hormone release, behaviour and milk production in dairy cows—further demonstrated by different milking routines. *Journal of Dairy Sciences* 2000.

Keverne, E. B. Central mechanisms underlying the neural and neuroendocrine determinants of maternal behaviour. *Psychoendocrinology* 1988:113, 127–141.

Nissen, E., et al. Different patterns of oxytocin, prolactin but not cortisol release during breastfeeding in women delivered by caeserean section or by the vaginal route. *Early human development* 1996:45, 103–118.

Nissen, E., et al. Oxytocin, prolactin, milk production and their relationship with personality traits in women after vaginal delivery or cesarean section. *Journal of Psychosomatic Obstetric and Gynaecology* 1998:19, 49–58.

Pedersen, C. A., et al. Oxytocin induced maternal behaviour in virgin maternal rats. *Science* 1982:216, 648–649.

Uvnäs Moberg, K. The neuroendocrinology of the mother-child interaction. *Trends in Endocrinology and Metabolism* 1966:7, 126–131.

Uvnäs Moberg, K., et al. Personality traits in women 4 days postpartum and their correlation with plasma levels of oxytocin and prolactin. *Journal of Obstetrics & Gynecology* 1990:11 261–273.

Uvnäs Moberg, K., and M. Eriksson. Breastfeeding: Physiological, endocrine and behavioural adaptations caused by oxytocin and local neurogenic activity in the nipple and the mammary gland. *Acta Paediatrica Scandinavica* 1996:85, 525–530.

Chapter 10: Oxytocin and Other Senses

Ågren, G., et al. The oxytocin antagonist 1-deamino–2-D-Tyr(Oet)–4-Thr–8-Orn-oxytocin reverses the increase in the withdrawal response latency to thermal, but not mechanical nociceptive stimuli following oxytocin administration or massage-like stroking in rats. *Neuroscience Letters* 1995:187, 49–52.

Ågren, G., K. Uvnäs Moberg, and T. Lundeberg. Olfactory cues from an oxytocin-injected male rat can induce antinociception in its cage mates. *Neuroreport* 1997:8, 3073–3076.Cruz, R., and M. Del Cerro. Role of the vomeronasal input in maternal behaviour. *Psychoneuroendocrinology* 1998:23, 905–926.

Cruz, R., and M. Del Cerro. Role of the vomeronasal input in maternal behaviour. *Psychoneuroendocrinology* 1998:23, 905–926.

Sato, A. Neural mechanisms of somatic sensory regulation of catecholamine secretion from the adrenal gland. *Advances in Biophysical Research* 1987:23, 39–80.

Stock, S., and K. Uvnäs Moberg. Increased plasma levels of oxytocin in response to afferent electrical stimulation of the sciatic and vagal nerves and in response to touch and pinch in anaestetized rats. *Acta Physiologica Scandinavica* 1998:132, 29–34.

Uvnäs Moberg, K., B. Posloncec, and L. Åhlberg. Influence on plasma levels of somatostatin, gastrin, glucagon, insulin and VIP-like immunoreactivity in peripheral venous blood of anesthetized cats induced by low intensity afferent stimulation of the sciatic nerve. *Acta Physiologica Scandinavica* 1986:126, 225–230.

Uvnäs Moberg, K., et al. Vagally mediated release of gastrin and cholecystokinin following sensory stimulation. *Acta Physiologica Scandinavica* 1992:146, 349–356.

Uvnäs Moberg, K., et al. The antinociceptive effect of non-noxious sensory stimulation is partly mediated through oxytocinergic mechanisms. *Acta Physiologic Scandinavica* 1993:149, 199–204.

Chapter 11: Oxytocin and Sexuality

Agmo, A., R. Andersson, and C. Johansson. Effect of oxytocin on sperm numbers in spontaneous rat ejaculates. *Biology and Reproduction* 1978,18 346–353.

Argiolas, A., and L. Gessa. Central functions of oxytocin. *Neuroscience and Biobehavioural Reviews* 1991:15, 217–231.

Arletti, R., and A. Bertolini. Ocytocin stimulates lordosis behaviour in female rats. *Neuropeptides* 1985:6, 247–255.

Bodansky, M., and L. E. Stanford. Oxytocin and the lifespan of male rats. *Nature* 1966.

Carmichael, M. S., et al. Plasma oxytocin increases in human sexual response. *Journal of Clinical Endocrinology and Metabolism* 1987:64, 27–31.

Carter, C. S. Oxytocin and sexual behaviour. *Neuroscience and Biobehavioural Reviews* 1992:16, 131–144.

Carter, C. S., A. C. De Vries, and L. L. Getz. Physiological substrates of mammalian monogamy: The prairie vole model. *Neuroscience and Biobehavioural Reviews* 1995:19, 303–314.

Hillegaart, V., et al. Sexual motivation promotes oxytocin secretion in male rats. *Peptides* 1988:19, 39–45.

Knight, T. W., and D. R. Lindsay. Short- and long-term effects of oxytocin on quality and quantity of semen from rams. *Journal of Reproduction and Fertility* 1970:21, 523–529.

Kumar, H., and N. K. Srivastava. Effect of oxytocin on the conception rate in rural bovines. *Indian Veterinary Medical Journal* 1994:18, 98–100.

Levin, K. L. The influence of oxytocin and proserin on the increase of sperm production in boars. *Veterinarija* 1968:43, 96–97.

Melin, P., and J. E. Kihlstrom. Influence of oxytocin on sexual behaviour in male rabbits. *Endocrinology* 1986:73, 433–435.

Chapter 12: Oxytocin and Relationships

Caldji, Ch., et al. Maternal care during infancy regulates the development of neural systems mediating the expression of fearfulness in the rat. *Proceedings of the National Academy of Sciences* 1998:95, 5335–5340.

Christensson, K., et al. Separation distress call in the human neonate in the absence of maternal body contact. *Acta Paediatrica* 1995:84, 468–473.

Field, T. M., S. M., Schanberg, and F. Scafadi. Tactile/kinesthetic stimulation effects on preterm neonates. *Pediatrics* 1986:77, 654.

Kennell, J. H., and M. H. Klaus. Bonding: Recent observations that alter perinatal care. *Pediatrics in Review* 1998:19, 4–12.

Klaus, M. H., et al. Maternal attachment: Importance of the first post-partum days. *New England Journal of Medicine* 1972:286, 460–463.

Klaus, M. H., J. H. Kennell, and P. H. Klaus. *The Doula Book.* Cambridge, Mass.: Perseus Publishing, 2002.

Knox, S., and K. Uvnäs Moberg. Social isolation and cardiovascular disease: An atherosclerotic connection. *Psychoneuroendocrinology* 1998:23, 877–890.

Komisaruk, B. R., and B. Whipple. Love as sensory stimulation: Physiological consequences of its deprivation and expression. *Psychoneuroendocrinology* 1998:23, 927–944.

Meaney, M. J., and D. H. Aitken. The effects of early postnatal handling on glucocorticoid receptor concentrations: Temporal parameters. *Developmental Brain Research* 1985:22, 301–304.

Panksepp, J., L. Normansell, and B. Herman. Neural and neurochemical control of the separation distress call. I: *The physiological control of mammalian vocalization* (ed.: J. D. Newman). New York: Plenum, 1998, 263–299.

Pauk, J., et al. Positive effects of tactile versus kinesthetic or vestibular stimulation on neuroendocrine and ODC activity in maternally-deprived rat pups. *Life Sciences* 1986:39, 2081–2087.

Porges, S. W. Love: An emergent property of the mammalian autonomic nervous system. *Psychoneuroendocrinology* 1998:23, 837–861.

Uvnäs Moberg, K., et al. Release of GI hormones in mother and infant by sensory stimulation. *Acta Paediatrica Scandinavica* 1987:76, 851–860.

Uvnäs Moberg, K. Physiological and endocrine effects of social contact. *Annals of New York Academy of Sciences* 1997:807, 146–163.

———. Oxytocin may mediate the benefits of positive social interaction and contact. *Psychoneuroendocrinology* 1998:23, 819–835.

Widstrom, A-M., et al. Short-term effects of early suckling and touch of the nipple on maternal behaviour. *Early Human Development* 1990:21, 153–163.

Williams, J. R., et al. Oxytocin centrally administered facilitates formation of a partner preference in female prairie voles (Microtus ochrogaster). *Journal of Neuroendocrinology* 1994:6, 247–250.

Witt, D. M., J. T. Winslow, and T. R. Insel. Enhanced social interactions in rats following chronic, centrally infused oxytocin. *Pharmacology, Biochemistry, and Behaviour* 1992:43, 855–861.

Chapter 13: Massage

Field, T., et al. Massage reduces anxiety in child and adolescent phychiatric patients. *Journal of the American Academy of Child Adolescence* 1992:31, 125–131.

Field, T. Massage therapy effects. *American Psychologist* 1998:53, 1270–1281.

von Knorring, A. L., A. Söderberg, L. Austin, H. Arinell, and K. Uvnäs Moberg. Massage induces decrease of aggressive behaviour in pre-school children. A long-term pilot study. *Journal of the American Academy of Child Adolescent Psychiatry*. Submitted.

Lund, I., et al. Sensory stimulation reduces blood pressure in unanaesthetized rats. *Journal of the Autonomic Nervous System* 1999:78, 30–37.

Uvnäs Moberg, K., et al. Stroking of the abdomen causes decreased locomotor activity in conscious male rats. *Physiology and Behaviour* 1996:60, 1409–1411.

Chapter 14: Eating: An Internal Massage

Field, T., and E. Goldson. Pacifying effects of non-nutritive sucking on term and pre-term neonates during heelstick procedures. *Pediatrics* 1984:74, 1012–1015.

Lindén, A., et al. Stimulation of maternal behaviour in rats with cholecystokinin octapeptide. *Journal of Neuroendocrinology* 1989:1, 389–392.

Nowak, R., et al. Cholecystokinin receptors mediate the development of a preference for the mother by newly born lambs. *Behavioural Neuroscience* 1997:11, 1375–1382.

————. Development of a preferential relationship with the mother by the newborn lamb: Importance of the sucking activity. *Physiology and Behaviour* 1997:62, 681–688.

Uvnäs Moberg, K. The gastrointestinal tract in growth and reproduction. *Scientific American* 1989:7, 78–83.

Uvnäs Moberg, K., G. Marchini, and J. Winberg. Plasma cholecystokinin concentrations after breastfeeding in healthy 4-day-old infants. *Applied Animal Behaviour* 1993:68, 46–48.

Uvnäs Moberg, K. Role of efferent and afferent vagal nerve activity during reproduction: Integrating function of oxytocin on metabolism and behaviour. *Psychoneuroendocrinology* 1994:19, 687–695.

Wells, A., et al. Influence of fat and carbohydrate on postprandial sleepiness, mood and hormones. *Physiology and Behaviour* 1997:61, 679–686.

Chapter 15: Cigarettes, Alcohol, and Other Drugs

Kovács, G. L., Z. Sarnyai, and G. Szabo. Oxytocin and addiction: A review. *Psychoneuroendocrinology* 1998: 23, 945–962.

Lindman, R. E., et al. Hormonal covariates of socioemotional communication as a function of assertiveness, gender and alcohol. Seventh Congress of the International society for biomedical research on alcoholism. Queensland, Australia 1994.

Uvnäs Moberg, K., et al. Low doses of ethanol may induce anti-nociceptive effects via an oxytocinergic mechanism. *Acta Physiologic Scandinavica* 1993:149, 117–118.

Chapter 16: Medication-Induced Calm and Connection

Alfvén, G., B. de la Torre, and K. Uvnäs Moberg. Depressed concentrations of oxytocin and cortisol in children with recurrent abdominal pain of non-organic origin. *Acta Paediatrica Scandinavica* 1994:83, 1076–1080.

Anderberg, U. M., and K. Uvnäs Moberg. Oxytocin levels decreased in high pain, stressful and depressive states within subgroups of female fibromyalgia patients. *Annals of Rheumatoid Diseases* 2000.

Arletti, R., and A. Bertolini, A. Oxytocin acts as an antidepressant in two animal models of depression. *Life Sciences* 1987: 41, 1725–1730.

Barker, D. J. P. In utero programming of chronic disease. *Clinical Sciences* 1998:95, 115–128.

Björkstrand, E., et al. The oxytocin receptor antagonist 1-deamino–2-D-Tyr-(OET)–4-Thr–8-Orn oxytocin inhibits effects of the 5 HT 1a receptor agonist 8 OH-DPAT on plasma levels of insulin, cholecystokinin and somatostatin. *Regulatory Peptides* 1996:63, 47–52.

Frasch, A., et al. Reduction of plasma oxytocin levels in patients suffering from major depression. *Advances in Experimental Medical Biology* 1995: 257–258.

Sohlström, A., C. H. Carlsson, and K. Uvnäs Moberg. Oxytocin treatment in early life counteracts some of the adverse effects of maternal undernutrition in rats. *Biology of the Neonate* 2000.

Uvnäs Moberg, K., et al. Personality traits in a group of individuals with functional disorders of the gastrointestinal tract and their correlation with gastin, somatostatin and oxytocin levels. *Journal of Psychosomatic Research* 1991:35, 515–533.

Uvnäs Moberg, K., et al. Oxytocin as a possible mediator of SSRI induced anti-depressant effects. *Psychopharmacology* 1999:142, 95–101.

Uvnäs Moberg, K., P. Alster, and T. Svensson. Amperozide and clozapine but not haloperidol or raclopride increase the secretion of oxytocin in rats. *Psychoparmacology* 1992:109, 473–476.

Uvnäs Moberg, K., et al. High doses of oxytocin cause sedation and low doses cause an anxiolytic-like effect in male rats. *Pharmacology, Biochemistry & Behaviour* 1994:49, 101–106.

Uvnäs Moberg, K., et al. Effects of 5-HT agonists selective for different receptor subtypes on oxytocin, CCK, gastrin and somatostatin plasma levels in the rat. *Neuropharmacology* 1996:35, 1635–1640.

Wakshlak, K. A., and M. Weinstock. Neonatal handling reverses behavioural abnormalities induced in rats by prenatal stress. *Physiology and Behaviour* 1990:48, 288–292.

Chapter 17: Motion and Stillness

Benson, H. Hypnosis and the relaxation response. *Gastroenenterology* 1989:96, 1609–1611.

Benson, H. Mind over maladies. Can yoga, prayer and meditation be adapted for medical care? *Hospitals & Health Networks* 1996:100, 212–216.

_____. The relaxation response: Therapeutic effect. *Science* 1997:278, 1694–1695.

_____. *The Relaxation Response: Updated and Expanded.* New York: Avon, 2000.

Hoffman, P., P. Thorén, and D. Ely. Effect of voluntary exercise on open field behaviour and on aggression in the spontaneously hypertensive rat (SHR). *Behavioral and Neural Biology* 1987:47, 346–355.

Hoffman, P., and P. Thorén. Electric muscle stimulation in the hind leg of the spontaneously hypertensive rat induces a long lasting fall in blood pressure. *Acta Physiologica Scandinavica* 1988:133, 211–219.

Myers, S. S., and H. Benson. Psychological factors in healing: A new perspective on an old debate. *Behavioural Medicine* 1992:18, 5–11.

Uvnäs Moberg, K., et al. The antinociceptive effect of non noxious sensory stimulation is partly mediated through oxytocinergic mechanisms. *Acta Physiologica Scandinavica* 1993:149, 199–204.

INDEX

About the Author, Translator, and Illustrator ✍

Kerstin Uvnäs Moberg, M.D., Ph.D., is recognized as a world authority on oxytocin. Her research takes place at the famed Karolinska Institute in Stockholm, and at the Swedish University of Agricultural Sciences in Uppsala, where she is Professor of Physiology. The author of more than 400 scientific papers and a previous book, *She and He,* Dr. Uvnäs Moberg lectures widely in Europe and the United States. Her work has been influential in a variety of fields, including obstetrics, psychology, animal husbandry, physical therapy, pediatrics, and child development. The mother of four children, she lives in Djursholm, Sweden.

Roberta W. Francis, writer and translator, works professionally on issues of racial and gender equality. A chance meeting with Kerstin Uvnäs Moberg on a flight to Sweden led to her participation in a 1997 Stockholm conference "Is There a Neurobiology of Love?" and to this translation. Roberta Francis lives in Chatham, New Jersey.

Airi Iliste is a graphic designer in Stockholm whose work has appeared in books, magazines, newspapers, and animated films. Her web site is www.airi.se.

ABOUT PINTER & MARTIN

Pinter & Martin is an independent book publisher based in London, with distribution throughout the world. We specialise in psychology, pregnancy, birth and parenting, fiction and yoga, and publish authors who challenge the status quo, such as Elliot Aronson, Grantly Dick-Read, Ina May Gaskin, Sheila Kitzinger, Stanley Milgram, Guillermo O'Joyce, Michel Odent, Gabrielle Palmer, Stuart Sutherland and Frank Zappa.

For more information visit www.pinterandmartin.com

05107113